D0482533

"Peter Hirsch presents to us the ultimate personification of success. His insightful section on The Purpose of Jesus will literally transform those who honestly read it and apply its immortal principles. . . . Peter is uniquely gifted in stripping the mystery away from profound truths and serving them up to the reader in concise and easily digestible realities. His book is simply glorious and gloriously simple. Countless lives will be indelibly impacted by this dynamic book."

Dr. Jerry L. Spencer
PAST PRESIDENT, SOUTHERN BAPTIST CONVENTION, PASTOR'S CONFERENCE

"Gripping from the first page; life changing if you apply its insights, this readable adventure cuts through confusion and reveals what you and I should do next."

John Dawson
FOUNDER, INTERNATIONAL RECONCILIATION COALITION

"The moment you meet Peter you are delightfully confronted and challenged by his passion: passion to learn, passion to grow, and passion to change. In *Success by Design* Peter not only proves that passion is within our reach, but actually transfers passion from his heart into ours. This book will help you make life count and do something of lasting significance."

Gerald Brooks
SENIOR PASTOR, GRACE OUTREACH CENTER, PLANO, TEXAS

"We yearn for success and significance. Unfortunately, we often pursue them in all the wrong ways. *Success by Design* shows us how to achieve these things on God's terms and in a way that is not only personally rewarding, but that blesses others. The Kingdom principles Peter Hirsch shares are eternal, practical, and available to everyone who wants to reach for all that life has to offer!"

Bill McCartney
FOUNDER AND PRESIDENT, PROMISE KEEPERS

"Peter Hirsch shows us how to let go, and let God change the meaning of our lives by design, rather than delusion. A value-packed book to underline and implement."

Dr. Denis Waitley
AUTHOR OF *SEEDS OF GREATNESS*

SUCCESS *by* DESIGN

TEN BIBLICAL SECRETS TO HELP YOU

ACHIEVE YOUR GOD-GIVEN POTENTIAL

Dr. Peter Hirsch

BETHANYHOUSE
MINNEAPOLIS, MINNESOTA

Published by Bethany House Publishers
A Ministry of Bethany Fellowship International
11400 Hampshire Avenue South
Bloomington, Minnesota 55438
www.bethanyhouse.com

Printed in the United States of America

Library of Congress Cataloging-in-Publication Data

Hirsch, Peter, 1965–
    Success by design : ten biblical secrets to help you achieve your God-given potential / by Peter Hirsch.
        p.   cm.
ISBN 0-7642-2634-7
    1. Success—Religious aspects—Christianity. I. Title.
    BV4598.3 .H57   2002
    248.4—dc21   2001005673

For Diana—

Who prayed me in . . .
I love you.

About the Author

Peter Hirsch worked his way up to the heights of business and personal success. Then he met Jesus, and his life was forever changed.

Born to a devout Jewish family, Peter studied in yeshivas (schools of advanced Jewish learning) for many years in both the United States and Israel. After receiving a law degree, he worked for a prestigious law firm, then discovered he had no passion for practicing law. Since 1992 Peter has consulted for many Fortune 500 companies and developed sales organizations. As president of Peter Hirsch International, he is an in-demand motivational speaker and sales trainer around the world.

He and his family live in Dallas, Texas, where he is a rabbi on staff at Baruch HaShem Synagogue, one of the largest Messianic synagogues in the world.

For more information about Peter Hirsch and *Success by Design*, please go to his Web site: *www.peterhirsch.org.*

Acknowledgments

To all those who continued to pray for me when all looked hopeless: Thank you for your persistence.

To Jenny and Sarah: You add constant joy and blessing to my life. What gifts of God you are!

To Scott Olson, David Easterbrook, Ken Ventura, and Janet Marshall: Your love, prayers, and reviews helped see this project through.

To Sandy and Paul Morris: Thanks for the suggestion referred to in *The Beginning.* It's good to have friends who have "been there and done that."

To Pastor Tommy Barnett: What a tremendous blessing your words have been in my life. May revival continue in Phoenix, led by Phoenix First Assembly.

To Zig Ziglar, Laurie Magers, James Robison, and Carol Stertzer: Thank you for your kind words of encouragement and support.

To Eddie and Josie Manansala: Thank you for your never-ending prayers, love, and faith.

To Pastor Gerald Brooks and the staff at Grace Outreach Center: I will never forget the kindness all of you showed and the growth in me that began with you.

To Russ Devan: A good friend and business trainer whose company name inspired the title of this book.

To Steve Laube, Sharon Madison, and the staff at Bethany House Publishers: It is a privilege to work with all of you.

To Claudia Cross: Thank you for your faith, vision, and patience.

To Marty and Marlene Waldman, and the entire staff and congregation at Baruch HaShem Synagogue: What a blessing it is to be a part of your family. Thank you for welcoming Diana, Jenny, and me into your hearts and homes. May God continue to pour out His blessing on us.

Contents

Foreword

Success by Design is a book that shares with all of us some steps we should take and why we should take them. Written by a committed member of the Jewish faith, who is also a born-again believer, this is a book that gives clear insights, thoughts, and directions that will make a difference in anyone's life.

It's common sense, biblically based, written from the heart, based on personal experience, and a study of God's Word. The author, as the saying goes, has "been there and done that." Now he wants you to come along with him. Not only does he want you to, but he also gives compelling reasons why the approach he's taking will enrich and enhance every phase of your life, making you a happier, healthier, better person as you battle the difficulties that very frequently come with life.

The biblical principles Peter Hirsch examines have worked for thousands of years, and we have every reason to believe they will continue to work. As a matter of fact, when I adopted many of these principles that Peter discusses with such passion, every facet of my life was affected and enriched.

I encourage you to pick up your pen when you pick up this book. Mark the passages that have meaning for you. Pause, reflect on, and pray about them. Then write yourself a little note, a reminder of something you can use that will make you a better person and a more complete human being—one able to harness the power God has instilled in you.

I encourage you not to pick up this book with the intention of "finishing" it, but rather read the book with the purpose of gleaning from it wisdom that will enrich your life increasingly with every subsequent reading. The enrichment begins when you begin to follow the directions and suggestions. So take the steps Peter Hirsch is encouraging you to take, and I really will see you—not just at the top, but over the top!

Zig Ziglar

The Beginning

The Bottom Line of Success

I was a success. By almost any definition, I had it made. My wife, Diana, and I were living on the island of Kauai, Hawaii. My office in my home had direct access to the balcony. Looking over my desk through the windows or doors, I had a complete, unobstructed view of both the mountains and the ocean. A few times a month I would travel for a few days, giving talks on success strategies and positive thinking to companies in different parts of the world. Life was grand. My family life was better than ever. All in all, I had achieved the American dream. And, of course, I had accomplished it all by myself. No one helped me—least of all, God.

Then one evening as my wife and I were sitting on the deck, holding hands and watching the sunset, enjoying the peace of island living, Diana said, "Sweetie, we're so blessed. We really need to thank Jesus for all these blessings."

My response was immediate: "Thank Jesus?!? You should thank me! I'm the one who worked my heart out so we could live like this!"

Diana simply smiled, said, "Okay," and took five steps back to avoid the lightning strike.

And lightning did indeed strike.

But you need to know the beginning of the story.

I was raised, and still am, a committed Jew. I studied in yeshivas (schools of Jewish learning) both in the United States and in Israel for many years. To me, Jesus was nothing more than a Jew who had gone wrong—a false prophet, at best. There was no place in me and in my Judaism for Jesus. Diana knew this. For three years she prayed for me, as did her family, every morning and evening, that I would find a relationship with Jesus. So when Diana suggested I thank Jesus, it was not quite a suggestion to which I was open.

Then came the lightning strike. Against my better judgment, I accepted a position to take over a company in Dallas after new investors had purchased it. The promises were huge. They would take it public, and I would shortly have more money than I needed for my grandchildren to retire—and I was only thirty-three years old! I didn't perform any personal due diligence on the company or its new owners, who turned out to be much less than completely honest. After less than four months, I realized this was not a situation to be in, and I left the company. Four months—I had escaped with my integrity intact—no harm done.

Or so I thought.

Six months later the Federal Trade Commission sued me. I couldn't believe it. A five-year-old company—I was only there four months—and the new owners weren't even sued. Just the old owner, a former employee, and me. Why? It didn't make any sense to me. Of course, it turned out to be one of the greatest things that ever happened to me, but I didn't see it that way at the time.

All I saw was that a powerful branch of the United States government had just sued me personally for 85 million dollars!

My "positive thinking" hit a wall. As much as I tried, I couldn't "positively think" my way out of this lawsuit. For the first time in my life, I was utterly powerless. If there was something I did wrong—no problem, let me correct it. But I didn't. I was simply in the wrong place at the wrong time, and there was nothing I could do about it. Days turned into weeks, which turned into months. There was no income coming in, and legal fees and other expenses were eating every dime of our savings. I had to move my family from a beautiful home on Kauai to a two-bedroom apartment in Dallas.

Depression hit, and it hit big. Still, Diana was nothing but supportive and loving. Her attitude never wavered. She was convinced that everything would be fine—that God would see us through this. Her "up" attitude drove me crazy! How could she be fine, when life was going down the drain? Looking back, I can now say that I was simply jealous of her calm. And I behaved how jealous people behave. I became angry and irrational. And went deeper into depression. I had those thoughts that many men have had at some point in their lives: *I'm worth more to my family dead than alive.* But my family wouldn't collect any insurance money if I committed suicide. So I had to make it look natural. For two straight weeks I couldn't sleep. I just didn't understand why this was happening to me. Finally, I came to what I now see as the greatest day of my life—a point of complete and total desperation. I had no way out—there were no positive options available to me. The prospect of one more sleepless night threw me into a fetal position on the floor, sobbing for hours.

Till this day I can't tell you why, but I got off the floor, and for the first time in my life I asked Jesus for help. Very simply, I said, "Jesus, if you're real, now is the time to show me, because there's not going to be a tomorrow. And I need help."

I can't quite articulate exactly what happened next. As best I can write it, I felt myself climb into bed, and it's as if two words were placed in my head. I didn't actually hear the words, but I felt them: *Trust me.* The amazing thing is, not only did I sleep through the night but I also woke up feeling at peace. It wasn't a lightning-bolt peace, but a simple, calm, life-changing peace that surpassed all my understanding. From that moment on, my life was no longer my own.

The change in me was dramatic, instant, and obvious. Everyone, from my attorney to my family and friends, asked, "What's wrong?"

I answered, "Absolutely nothing."

They replied, "But you seem so peaceful." To them, I was supposed to be a wreck. That's what I was until then, and that's the expectation I created. But I had a new not-so-secret power.

I made the commitment that I would never speak to a public audience again without giving my testimony. Yes, I would continue to speak about success principles, but I would base everything in my life, from my writing and speaking to my relationships, on the Word of God.

The United States government and the Federal Trade Commission didn't scare me anymore. I literally gave the entire situation up to my Father in heaven. After all, He was the one who could end it, not me.

At the advice of a friend, I even went so far as to change the caption on the lawsuit. It no longer read, "The Federal Trade

Commission against Peter Hirsch." On my copy, the caption read, "The Federal Trade Commission against Peter Hirsch (and 10,000 angels in heaven, all of my brothers and sisters in Christ, and my Lord and Savior Jesus Christ)." I literally wrote that in on my copy of the complaint. The visual impact was tremendous. No government in the history of the world could ever stand a chance against all that power.

I even followed Jesus' commandment and prayed for my enemies, the attorneys of the Federal Trade Commission. At first, I did it because Jesus said I should. The blessing went something like "Jesus, you say I should bless my enemies. I don't want to and don't even know if I mean it, but bless 'em. Amen." But soon the prayers became sincere, and I did pray for them to come to a closer relationship with Jesus and to know the peace and love that's available to them through that relationship. And as I prayed for them, I realized I was getting my own release. Praying for my enemies actually freed me from the bondage of my own negative thoughts. Powerful!

Diana was the first to point out that the lawsuit was a true blessing because it brought me to a relationship with Jesus. My initial reaction to that was "A vision would have been just fine." But the reality is, the lawsuit was a blessing. Issues in my life such as humility (or the lack thereof), gratitude (or the lack of it), pride, arrogance, conceit, and a host of others had to be dealt with. Plus, it was a pretty clear message that I needed to listen more to Diana. I absolutely believe that had I simply thanked Jesus that first time, when Diana asked me to, He could have dealt with me in a less dramatic way. I could just picture Father in heaven peering down over heaven's balcony, watching the scene as I refused to be thankful. With a half-smile and half-grin, He must have said, "Okay, Peter, you asked for it. You could have made it easier, but I guess you're choosing the long route. Well, here goes . . ."

Yes, the lawsuit was a blessing. Never again will I doubt the awesome power of our Father in heaven and the love He has for us.

Indeed, the celebration of that love, and all the success attached to it, has become my mission in life.

That others would learn to lead a life of *Success by Design*— God's design—has become my passion.

For, you see, success has been given many different definitions by many different people. But God has only one definition. In God's eyes, you are a success if you acknowledge that you are His child. That is the bottom line. Our Father wants us to be successful, and He has given us the blueprint. It's called the Bible. Every secret to leading a successful, passionate life is in the Bible. I am merely drawing your attention to it. And success is not about money. It doesn't matter how much money you have, what kind of car you drive, or what kind of house you live in. It doesn't matter whether you drive a truck or fly rockets. Here's what does matter: knowing that you are a child of God; knowing that He loves you; and knowing that He wants to bless you. God, through Jesus Christ, said, "I have come that they may have life, and that they may have it more abundantly" (John 10:10 NKJV).

For many of you, this seems silly and terribly naïve. I know. I used to think the same thing. But now I know without a doubt that true success will never come unless you *first* get yourself right with God through Jesus Christ. From this beginning, everything else in this book flows.

We've all heard it before: *God first.* It's true. If you implement any of the strategies that follow in this book without first getting right with God, you will have wasted your time as a reader and mine as a writer. So here's how it works: Get right with God, then implement the biblical secrets taught in this book. If you follow that order, I believe with all my heart success from God will begin to come your way.

SECRET 1

Challenge is a catalyst for success

Secret #1

Challenge

> *"With your help I can advance against a troop; with my God I can scale a wall."*
>
> PSALM 18:29

Have you ever reached a point in your life or work where you realized you were really not where you wanted to be?

Have you ever stopped and noticed that you could be doing more, achieving more, experiencing more success?

Have you ever wondered what it would be like to go beyond making *incremental* gains in your performance or in the quality of your life and work—to rocket past your previous limitations and make a real breakthrough?

That's the possibility of *Success by Design*. And it's all yours; all you have to do is develop the challenge and play with it.

Challenge is a catalyst for success.

I offer this book as a challenge. *Success* is a challenge. I challenge you to become all that you can be—and more. And even more than that, I challenge you to have a blast doing it!

Why do I make such an outlandish challenge? Because I want you to understand that meeting challenge head on is a joy.

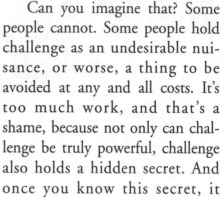

MEETING
CHALLENGE
HEAD ON
IS A JOY.

Can you imagine that? Some people cannot. Some people hold challenge as an undesirable nuisance, or worse, a thing to be avoided at any and all costs. It's too much work, and that's a shame, because not only can challenge be truly powerful, challenge also holds a hidden secret. And once you know this secret, it makes all the challenges you face in your life and work a joy to deal with.

Ready? Here it is:

A challenge is NOT THE TRUTH.

Challenge literally means "false accusation." Trace the word back through the Middle English *calenge* and Old French *chalenge*, all the way to the Latin *calumniari*—and they all turn out to mean "accuse falsely."

That means a challenge is simply *not the truth*; it's something that's made up.

The truth is, we *make up* challenges to serve our needs, our desires, and our purposes. Thus, a challenge is something that is *not yet* true. It is not a lie, but a dream, a hope, an obstacle to overcome, but one that has *not yet* been achieved.

That puts a new light on challenge, doesn't it?

So when I use the word *challenge* in this book, I'm clear that I'm making it up to serve my mission, which is to have millions of people living a life of *Success by Design* through a relationship with and commitment to our Lord Jesus Christ and through the success principles He teaches us in the Bible.

The greatest challenges you can develop are challenges that inspire you. Don't bother with challenges that serve only to distract or frustrate you. Remember that *challenges are not the truth*—so you get to choose whether to entertain them or not.

Discard any challenges in your life that don't inspire and encourage you, that do not serve your ability to choose *Success by Design*.

I used to avoid challenges—or attempt to. Not anymore. In my life today, I actively seek challenges, ferret them out, make them up whenever I can, because I've caught on to their power to give me power. I'm a connoisseur of fine challenges—a challenge nut. "My name is Peter. I am a challengeaholic." And I recommend you be the same.

Probably no other football coach in history was as successful as the legendary Vince Lombardi of the Green Bay Packers, who coached a successful career, then retired, and then came back to coach again. One of his legions of admirers, Tommy Prothro, said that he, too, would "like to win every game, but I'm not sure winning would mean much if I always won. I think that's why Vince quit. He'd won too much. He came back because he missed it, but by then he had a new challenge—making a comeback."

One of the greatest perceived challenges given in biblical times was the challenge God gave to the ancient Hebrews before they entered the land of Israel. "See, the Lord your God *has given you* the land. Go up and take possession of it as the Lord, the God of your fathers, told you. Do not be afraid; do not be discouraged" (Deuteronomy 1:21, emphasis added). Do you see by looking carefully at the emphasized words "has given you" that the challenge was really a figment of the people's imagination? The Hebrews had two choices. They could have accepted God at His word and confidently taken the land. That would have been a good choice. Unfortunately, the people made the other choice. Rather than believe God, they believed a few spies who said that the land would be impossible to conquer. They *made up* a negative challenge that was absolutely not the truth. And that cost them years of trouble.

On the other hand, there is King David, who made up challenges to inspire him. Before he was crowned king, a giant of a man named Goliath, the Philistine, who was over nine feet tall, challenged the people of Israel: "Choose a man and have him come down to me. If he is able to fight and kill me, we will become your subjects; but if I overcome him and kill him, you will become our subjects and serve us" (1 Samuel 17:8–9). Nobody wanted to be a Philistine slave. The people were understandably a bit nervous. But not David. David was strengthened by these words. He said to the giant, "You come against me with sword and spear and javelin, but I come against you in the name of the Lord Almighty, the God of the armies of Israel, whom you have defied. This day the Lord will hand you over to me, and I'll strike you down and cut off your head" (1 Samuel 17:45–46). God did, and so did David. David "ran quickly toward the battle line to meet him" (1 Samuel 17:48). David knew that Goliath's challenge was not really a challenge at all but something the Israelites had made up because they lacked the faith David possessed. David knew that running away from battles is the one sure way to keep them coming after us. How many of us are making up our own Goliaths?

Accepting a positive challenge has a powerful and lifelong impact not only on we who accept the challenge but also on many around us. When Jesus said to His first two disciples,

Simon called Peter and his brother Andrew, "Come, follow me . . . and I will make you fishers of men," do you remember what they did? They immediately accepted the positive challenge. "At once they left their nets and followed him" (Matthew 4:19–20). And the world has never been the same since.

A routine of constant challenge builds strong beings in much the same way that a good gym workout builds strong bodies.

Challenge makes you strong by exercising your creative mental and emotional muscles. Challenge tones your intuition and imagination, exercises your desire, puts mass on your positive beliefs, trims your fears, and adds definition and articulation to your attitudes. Challenges are the free weights you use to train for success.

If you're ready, let's go! Name your life challenge and move to the next step on the way to success. A challenge is meaningless without the *belief* to make it happen. Let's go there now.

SECRET 2

Belief is being certain of possibilities

Secret #2

Belief

A s we New York Mets fans used to say during the 1969 and 1973 baseball seasons: "You just gotta believe."

Belief is a feeling of certainty—but being certain of what?

Being certain of possibilities.

When we believe something, what we really believe is that a thing is *possible*. Life after death, a cure for cancer or lupus or AIDS, success in any endeavor—we either believe it's possible or we don't. "Impossibility" might simply be defined as "the absence of positive belief."

Jesus made it quite clear: "I have come into the world as a light, so that no one who believes in me should stay in darkness" (John 12:46). The more *certain* you feel a thing is possible for you, the stronger will be your belief and the less darkness you will have. Conversely, you can weaken or even kill a belief by introducing *doubt*.

Doubt is like black paint. Belief is white. Have you ever mixed white paint into black to get gray? It takes an extraordinary amount of white added to black to lighten it, yet the tiniest dab of black added to white makes it gray immediately. Doubt is like that.

Scripture puts it this way: "He who doubts is like a wave of the sea, blown and tossed by the wind" (James 1:6).

While we must fight doubt, understand that it is a normal reaction. After all, John the Baptist had doubts about Jesus! Even after John heard the voice from heaven immediately following Jesus' baptism, John sent people to question whether Jesus was "the one who was to come, or should we expect someone else?" (Luke 7:19). John's doubts have their roots in the widely held Jewish messianic expectations of that time. Most Jews were looking for and expecting a King David-like messiah who would bring freedom from Rome. Of course, Jesus did come to bring freedom, but not necessarily political freedom. If John were looking for a messiah who would comfort the needy and bring freedom from sin, he would not have had doubts. Clearly, doubts have much to do with our expectations. The point is simple: We must never let doubts in our heads rob us of faith in our hearts.

For over one hundred years the Holy Grail of athletic competition was to run a mile in less than four minutes. Yet with each failed attempt, the possibility of success faded further—not simply further into the future, but further from any possibility whatsoever.

In the '20s, '30s, '40s, and early '50s, science and what passed for sports medicine held that the human body was simply incapable of such unbelievable performance. The conventional wisdom of the day was that the lungs could not process enough oxygen to sustain the effort; they would burst under the strain, as would the heart. The bones would fracture, joints rupture, muscles give out, ligaments and tendons tear and fail under such stress. It was a physiological and psychological barrier. A human being running a mile in under four minutes was just *not possible.*

Until May 6, 1954, in Oxford, England—when a young medical student named Roger Bannister ran a mile in 3 minutes, 59.4 seconds.

Obviously Bannister believed it was possible—and with his historic run he broke not only the physical four-minute barrier but also a universally held "belief barrier." Within another three years another runner had duplicated Bannister's feat—and in the years that followed hundreds of others did it, too!

What were they all waiting for?

Today *thousands* of runners around the world have run a mile in under four minutes. They even do it in high school! Bannister proved it was possible. Now *everyone* believes it. "Impossible" is also something we *make up.*

"Whatever you ask for in prayer, believe that you have received it, and it will be yours" (Mark 11:24). If only He hadn't said, "Believe." If only we could just *get* whatever we ask for. Jesus is teaching us something very important for our growth. When we doubt, we stifle our ability to reach our potential.

Clearly belief is powerful!

Your Beliefs Are Your Destiny

"In the beginning God created the heavens and the earth" (Genesis 1:1). Your belief in the first sentence of the Bible is likely to determine your beliefs in virtually every area of your life. Here we are confronted with a serious choice of what to believe. Do we believe the evolutionists or the Big Bang theorists, who say it all happened by chance? Do you believe prayer has no place in the public schools, or do you believe, as I do, that when prayer came out of our schools, guns went in? Do you believe that adultery is no big deal, or do you believe, as I do, that we shouldn't trust a man whose wife can't? Do you believe that "As for God, his way is perfect; the word of the Lord is flawless. He is a shield for all who take refuge in him" (2 Samuel 22:31), or do you believe we're here on our own? Either way, your beliefs will shape your destiny.

Your beliefs shape your actions. Your actions cause results, the circumstances of your life; and those results, when stretched out over a lifetime, are what is called *your destiny*. Therefore, your beliefs—what you cause your mind to think and feel certain about—are the causative source of your destiny.

Now, stop and think for a moment: Is that the way you think it works?

For many people, this is a dramatic shift in their way of thinking. Most of us walk around believing that when we earn that $100,000, or drive that Porsche, or live in that fantastic house—then we'll really feel great!

We think that results cause our feelings.

Well, it *can* work that way—but that's not the *only* way it has to be. Obviously things happen, and you feel one way or another about them. That's a choice you have. But do you see that *your feelings can also cause results?*

Remember, your beliefs are *feelings of certainty*—feelings which, however aware or unaware you might be of them, you choose to have. Your feelings direct your actions. So if you want to achieve a specific result, one surefire way to get it is to *feel* the way you would if that result were already present and true for you.

How would you feel if you earned $100,000? Can you think of any better way to bring that kind of income into your life as fast as possible than *feeling like a $100,000-income earner*? There isn't any.

How would you feel if you led hundreds of teenagers to a relationship with God? How would you feel if you led thousands of the poor and hurting to the saving knowledge of Jesus Christ?

Whether or not a big check or a life on the mission field happens to appeal to you, my point is just how powerful a tool belief can be. This is not "positive thinking" mumbo jumbo; it's how great accomplishments actually occur. It's how success happens. And it's crucial that you understand this point—or at least try it on as a *possibility*.

Now, knowing this is not enough. Knowledge alone never produces accomplishment. One of the greatest half-truths (i.e., half-lies!) in the world is "knowledge is power."

Not quite.

Do you remember from your high school science days the two types of energy: "potential" and "kinetic"? Potential energy is just that, potential. It just sits there, accomplishing nothing. Kinetic energy is *energy in action*. It's actually doing something.

It's the same with the energy of knowledge. Knowledge in action is kinetic. It's moving and shaking, not just sitting there in your mind.

And what quality breaks the inertia of potential knowledge's tendency to "just sit there," doing nothing, and turns it into wisdom in action?

Belief.

The #1 belief for all high-achievers I have ever met or studied is the belief that *action supercedes everything*.

I know this is another fundamental shift for many of us: it means changing the habitual strategy of "Ready, aim, fire" to the more proactive—and, most people would assume, more reckless and dangerous—"Fire, aim, ready!"

But that's precisely the kind of shift that generates quantum leaps and breakthroughs in our lives.

Action supercedes everything.

Two Types of Beliefs

Beliefs come in two forms: powerful or limiting, also referred to as possibility or no-possibility. People commonly refer to these as "positive" or "negative" beliefs.

All those runners had the "fact" that Sir Roger had already run a 3:59.4 mile to bolster their courage. But Bannister didn't. How did *he* form such a powerful belief, while the rest of the world held tenaciously to their limiting ones?

The answer is surprisingly simple: *He made it up.* He made up a challenge and then believed it would happen.

This is one of the great inspiring secrets to success in any and every aspect of life and work. You make up your beliefs. You decide. Positive or negative, you choose to believe what and how you do.

It's the possibility we *believe* in—and we discover possibilities even when we have the most limiting evidence at hand.

When the centurion said to Jesus, "Just say the word, and my servant will be healed" (Matthew 8:8), he believed that the physical presence of Jesus wasn't necessary for healing to occur. He had no proof. He just had his belief. And how did Jesus answer him? "Go! It will be done just as you believed it would" (Matthew 8:13). Clearly, powerful beliefs are rewarded.

We have a choice: develop beliefs that limit or develop

beliefs that inspire. It really is that simple.

Okay, so how do you do that?

First things first: *Don't try!*

Trying Is SO Trying

Since belief is a feeling of certainty based on possibility, and since it seems so very true that "man can only do what he believes he can do," this puts the kibosh on the word *try*.

See if there's a pen or pencil near you. Actually, any object will do. Now, *try* to pick it up.

What happened? If this doesn't make sense to you, then don't just read it—really, go ahead, *try*. Now, don't actually pick it up—that would be *doing*. Don't DO it, just *try* to do it. Do you see the difference? Doing is the action. Trying is inaction and procrastination. In the words of the *Star Wars* Jedi Knight Yoda, "Luke, you either do or you do not—there is no 'try'."

If your dictionary has the word *try* in it, I suggest you draw a big line through it. Then do the same with the *try* in your own vocabulary.

Now, let's get back to how to develop beliefs that give you power and how to rid yourself of limiting beliefs.

Asking the Right Questions

One thing I've found common to all the high-achievers I've met is that they ask themselves questions that help them develop beliefs that inspire and encourage.

For example, what kind of question is this? "Why am I so fat?"

Is it a limiting or a powerful question?

Look at the possibilities for an answer to that question.

They're all limiting: "Because I'm a pig." "I have no willpower." "I just can't stop eating." "My whole family is fat." No matter what you say, you're trapped. You're either a failure or a helpless victim—probably both.

But ask the question this way instead: "What action could I take to lose twenty pounds AND enjoy the process?"

Now what happens with your answer? You begin to explore the possibilities, don't you? You start looking at possible solutions, exploring new and inspiring ideas. Maybe you've even begun to make up some new beliefs for yourself.

It's a whole new and different ball game. It's a high-achieving question that can be answered only by high-achieving possibilities.

One key to establishing new beliefs in yourself—and in others, too—is to ask questions that elicit positive possibility answers.

For example: Turn "Why can't I quit smoking?" into a positive by asking, "What steps can I take to be smoke-free?" Or turn "What would I do if I lost my job?" into "What alternatives exist to give me the work security I want and deserve?"

In each of these instances, the answers shift from those that serve only to strengthen your negative beliefs and limitations of no possibility into those that strengthen your aspirations and desires and that generate new beliefs for what is possible for you to achieve.

Once two little kittens discovered a big pail of cream. Now, being kittens, they both tried everything they could to get to all that delicious cream. They finally did—and they fell in!

At first, they were both in kitty heaven, swimming around in the cream, lapping it up, drinking more and more and more. But after drinking their fill, they suddenly realized that they couldn't get out! They tried and tried, but the rim of the pail was just too high to reach.

About this time, their kitten playmates came along and gathered around the rim of the big pail, shouting and jeering at the two kittens in the cream. They made fun of them, mocked them, and laughed at how stupid and foolish they were to fall into the pail of cream, where they couldn't get out.

One kitten kept looking up at the others all making fun of him and felt more and more dejected. He kicked and flailed his legs and paws, but to no avail. Finally he gave up and sank exhausted into the cream.

But the other kitten kept looking up at her playmates. She seemed to be renewed by their taunts and kept trying to jump up and reach the edge of the pail. Eventually all her jumping about turned the cream to butter; she stood on the firm surface and jumped up and out of the pail easily.

When she got out and stood next to the other kittens, one of them leaned over and asked, "How come you kept trying, even though we were laughing at you and making fun of you and telling you you'd never make it?"

"Oh," replied the kitten in surprise, "you see, I'm a little deaf. I thought you were cheering me on—and that inspired me to keep trying."

Please understand that I absolutely do not believe in affirmations that are nothing more than lies; I do, however, believe in the power of encouragement.

Using the success secret "belief" means turning a kitten's deaf ear to any and all limiting beliefs you may encounter.

It's simply a numbers game. More bad news: limiting beliefs. More good news: powerful beliefs. And the best news of all is that we can each choose what news we get.

You've probably heard about the power of affirmations. They

work—and the reason they work so well is that they are simply positive talk that is sent into the subconscious on a regular basis; they literally reprogram the way you think and feel about yourself. But again, understand that lies don't work. If you're broke and don't want to be broke anymore, don't bother with affirmations saying, "I'm rich!" That's called delusion; it's a lie. If you're broke, the most powerful affirmation is "I'm broke, and I don't like it! It stops now! I'm done being broke!"

That's all you have to do to discover new, powerful beliefs in yourself. And it works for replacing limiting beliefs with positive, supportive messages, as well.

Although this is a truth people often forget, *you have control over what you think.* In fact, like the choice of what you believe, it is one of the very few things over which you truly do have control. What you think determines your beliefs, which dictate what is or is not possible for you to accomplish in your life.

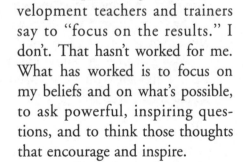

WHAT YOU
THINK
DETERMINES
YOUR BELIEFS.

Some personal growth and development teachers and trainers say to "focus on the results." I don't. That hasn't worked for me. What has worked is to focus on my beliefs and on what's possible, to ask powerful, inspiring questions, and to think those thoughts that encourage and inspire.

I prefer to leave the results up to the One who controls them: God. The rest, I think, is up to you and me.

Let me give you a powerful example: Jesus said, "Whoever believes in me, as the Scripture has said, streams of living water will flow from within him" (John 7:38). John then clarifies that Jesus is talking about the Holy Spirit. When you turn your life over to Jesus and you desire to live a life congruent with that decision, the Holy Spirit will guide you. We will discuss decision-making in greater detail in chapter 10. For now, since I understand that many of my readers will not have made the decision to live for Jesus, I will speak about intuition. In all fairness, though, I must warn you that intuition can be messy when we are not guided by correct principles. When we are guided by the love of our Father, through the Holy Spirit, we can trust our intuition. As King Solomon wrote, "Trust in the Lord with all your heart and lean not on your own understanding; in all your ways acknowledge him, and he will make your paths straight" (Proverbs 3:5–6). While God will certainly let us make our own mistakes—that's called free will—when we lean on God, our intuition is at its peak. "For great is His love toward us, and the faithfulness of the Lord endures forever" (Psalm 117:2).

It is your thoughts and feelings that inspire the results you accomplish in your life. When they are, in some unexplainable way, aligned with what is right and true, your thoughts and feelings simply proceed toward an inevitable conclusion that you call "the result."

Do you want to feel wonderful? Think wonderful. Don't assume that once certain hoped-for or anticipated results are achieved, the wonderful feeling will follow. That's the big lie. Positive thoughts and feelings are *not the result* of positive results. *They are the cause.*

Just try—remember that?—to walk around depressed, dejected, and angry at life for throwing dirt in your face and see what you get. More dirt! It just doesn't work any other way. Want dirt? Ask for it. Want gold instead? Change the question.

We'll refer to imagination later. It's a critical faculty—one of the mental exercises that keeps truly successful people's minds young and fresh. Imagination is one of our greatest and, sadly, least used resources. For some reason people assume imagination is the sole province of artists, children, and crazy people. Shakespeare put these words in the mouth of Duke Theseus:

> The lunatic, the lover, and the poet
> Are of imagination all compact:
> One sees more devils than vast hell can hold,
> That is, the madman: the lover, all as frantic,
> Sees Helen's beauty in a brow of Egypt:
> The poet's eye, in a fine frenzy rolling,
> Doth glance from heaven to earth, from earth to heaven;
> And as imagination bodies forth
> The forms of things unknown, the poet's pen
> Turns them to shapes and gives to airy nothing
> A local habitation and a name.
> —*A Midsummer Night's Dream*

But the duke had it wrong. We all have the gift of the poet, rich in the possibilities of boundless imagination—the ability to give shapes and names to things unknown, to dream. We just forget.

Just as intuition is not just for women, imagination is for all of us. But for most people, imagination is a "muscle" that's not used enough to be flexible and strong. So take it to the gym and give it a good workout a couple of times a week, and pretty soon your imagination will have biceps like Arnold Schwarzenegger.

A reporter was talking with Walt Disney's son at the grand opening of Disney World in Florida. The reporter said, "It's too bad Walt didn't live to see this."

Walt's son replied, "He did. That's why you're looking at it now."

Imagination. Powerful.

More powerful than ordinary beliefs are beliefs that cause us to take action without evidence. That's called living "by faith, not by sight" (2 Corinthians 5:7), and nothing is mightier. "The only thing that counts is faith expressing itself through love" (Galatians 5:6). When you put your faith in Jesus, nothing is impossible. And there is definitely a difference between faith and positive thinking. Put simply, faith focuses on God's ability to deal with your current situation, whatever that might be.

History has proven that one idea held with an unwavering faith is more powerful than 10,000 marching armies. Indeed, it is faith that enrolled the signatures of fifty-six men on the Declaration of Independence; it is faith that caused Martin Luther King Jr. to stand in front of a crowd of thousands and shout, "I have a dream!" And it is faith that caused the crashing of the Berlin wall. The whole history of mankind is a demonstration of the invincible power of an idea clothed in nothing but the truth and armed with the power of faith. "If you have faith as small as a mustard seed, you can say to this mountain, 'Move from here to there' and it will move. *Nothing will be impossible for you*" (Matthew 17:20, emphasis added). This is not a joke. Faith can and does move mountains!

Faith in Jesus Christ will sustain you in the most challenging times of your life. No matter what enemy comes against you, you will know you are protected. Do you remember what I wrote in the introduction, "The Beginning," about the government's complaint against me? "If we are thrown into the blazing furnace, the God we serve is able to save us from it" (Daniel 3:17). Don't think for a moment that I didn't feel as though I were being thrown into the furnace. And I know that many of you feel that way right now because of certain situations life is throwing your way. Please, I beg you, try it out. Ask Jesus for help and then trust Him.

Don't let anyone push, nudge, or shove you off course. Stand tall in your faith. "If you do not stand firm in your faith, you will not stand at all" (Isaiah 7:9). But when you DO stand firm, the world opens up to you. You become unstoppable. Listen to these words of Jesus: "I tell you the truth, anyone who has faith in me will do what I have been doing. He will do *even greater* things than these" (John 14:12, emphasis added). Just realize what Jesus had been doing—curing the sick and the lame and the blind, raising the dead—and know that through faith we can do *even greater* things. I know it's true. When I had reached that wonderful day of total and utter desperation, at my wit's end and with no options, *I was raised from the dead.* There is one thing we can do through faith that even Jesus himself could never do, no matter what! Jesus never could point to himself while speaking with others, and say, "Look at me, a sinner, saved by the blood of the Lamb." The power and strength of our testimonies can lead to the greatest of all miracles! Faith is that powerful.

In one of the most frightening experiences in Israel's history in the wilderness, hordes of poisonous snakes attacked the people. When Moses interceded on behalf of the Israelites, "The Lord said to Moses, 'Make a snake and put it up on a pole; anyone who is bitten can look at it and live.' So Moses made a bronze snake and put it up on a pole" (Numbers 21:8–9). God used the image of a brass snake as a tool of redemption. I am sure there were many who thought looking up at a bronze snake was too ridiculous to consider. Those people died. Those who had faith lived.

Jesus tells Nicodemus, "Just as Moses lifted up the snake in the desert, so the Son of Man must be lifted up, that everyone who believes in him may have eternal life" (John 3:14–15). Once again, God's uplifted form has the power to heal—this time not merely from poison but from all sin and death. All that's required is faith.

Just a few more things about faith: Faith works with wisdom; it doesn't replace wisdom. Faith does not mean that we know it all! "By faith Abraham, when called to go to a place he would later receive as his inheritance, obeyed and went, *even though he did not know where he was going*" (Hebrews 11:8, emphasis added). Also, having faith does not mean that the answer shows up right away. "*For he waited* for the city which has foundations, whose builder and maker is God" (Hebrews 11:10 NKJV, emphasis added). Instead, faith believes God is working even when we don't see Him working. Faith is believing in God's promises to the point that we know He will do what He promised. Remember Joshua and Caleb? They believed God would do what He promised and give Israel the land. They believed in the face of empirical evidence to the contrary. Why? Because they took God at His word, and they were rewarded.

All of us face the battle of reason versus faith. The biblical mandates to "bless those who curse you" and "give and it will be given to you" can appear utterly ridiculous. Of course, there are now enough testimonies of the strength, wisdom, and rewards that follow those mandates to believe they work, but without faith that the Bible is true, why would someone believe them in the first place?

Faith and belief are at their best when they evolve from and express two things all human beings need as much as air, water, and food: *purpose and values*. That's where we're going next.

3

SECRET

The people we are and every thing we do are inspired by our purpose and values

Secret #3

Purpose

I neeeeeeed a reason!" The reason why we are doing something—anything—is of utmost importance. If the reasons are clear, the rest will make itself known. People who know WHY they are doing something inevitably outperform people who know how; people who know how usually work for people who know why. Those with a purpose guide those without by instilling their purpose in them.

When Jesus saw a fig tree and discovered no figs on it, it was one of the few times He "lost His cool." Jesus said, "May you never bear fruit again!" (Matthew 21:19), and the fig tree immediately withered. No figs on a fig tree—unacceptable. What else is there for a fig tree to do than to bear figs? The fig tree wasn't living its purpose.

The people we are and every thing we do—both are inspired by our purpose and values.

Take a look at any trouble in the world: rival factions in a warring country, rivalry between corporate competitors, or an argument between a husband and wife who are not getting along: I can promise you'll find that the parties involved do not recognize or honor the other's values or encourage each other to express their life purpose.

Let's start with values first, because they are the seed from which purpose grows.

Values Are the Heart of the Matter

Your values are what make you tick. Your values are the seat and source of your wants and desires. Yet most people don't really think about their values—or the values of others, even when they're considering what it takes to be successful.

Whenever I'm speaking to someone about the possibility of coming into business with me, the first thing I look for is to discover what his or her values are. In fact, I base my relationships with people on their values and how they relate to me and to mine.

Our values are the wellspring from which comes all that we want in life, everything we seek after or search for. Our values are the source of who we think we are.

Let me give you an example of a value:

One of the most powerful values many people share in our world today is *belonging*. People want to belong, to be a part of what's going on and what's happening.

Did you know that there are over one hundred and twenty formal twelve-step groups operating in the United States today? People really want to belong—and they often want us to know who they are and what it is they belong to, as well. That's another value, which some marketers are now calling "egonomics."

Look at the T-shirts, athletic gear, and hats we buy—even if we've never shot a basket, run a mile, or sailed. These items have the brand names of the makers plastered all over them. These products do more than just advertise the manufacturer's name. They are statements of their owner's values.

Look at the license plates on our cars. Ten, fifteen years ago, they were meaningless combinations of letters and numbers. Today they say things like "BOBS AUDI," "BMW4MOM," "MYTOY," and "GOLFPRO."

Do you think a man or woman wearing a Rolex is expressing his or her values? That's pretty straightforward, right? Now look at this: I know a multimillionaire who wears a forty-eight dollar Timex because it's an expression of *his* values! He likes people to notice his inexpensive watch—and to know that he *could* wear anything, no matter how much it costs. One of his values is *being different*, another is *being thrifty*.

Values are so intrinsic to who we are that it's not really a matter of values being something we *choose to have*. It's almost as if we are showing what values *have us*. Values are that compelling.

Values motivate us. And when we find our values not being respected by certain people or institutions, we "disappear" them (the people and institutions, that is) like the stranger in Yosarian's tent in the novel *Catch-22*.

We will not keep company with people who do not honor our values. We will not do business with companies that do not respect the expression of our values.

Let me give you a famous example: Have you ever shopped at Nordstrom? Nordstrom is a very successful department store chain, and one reason it is so successful is that it is very big on honoring people's values. They play live piano music in their stores and serve food to shoppers. They bend over backward to have a "the customer is king, or queen" image. It is a real and tangible value for each of their current and potential customers.

Nordstrom also has one of the most liberal return policies in all of shoppingdom.

> One day an elderly woman came in and told a Nordstrom salesman that she wanted to return something that was out in her car. The sales clerk accompanied her to the parking lot and proceeded to unload four tires the lady was dissatisfied with. He promptly wrote up her credit, returned her money, thanked her for her patronage, and expressed the hope that she would return and find her future purchases more satisfactory.

Pretty good service, I'd say: true respect for the customer's values. Except for one thing: *Nordstrom has never sold tires!*

Respect my values and you've got a friend for life. Ignore them and . . .

What do you suppose is at the heart of the high divorce rate in the United States? What do you suppose would happen to the institution of marriage if all the he's and she's respected and supported each other's values? Yet how many husbands and wives truly know with clarity what each other's values are?

Values are bottom line.

So what are *your* values? What qualities do you most admire and most want to experience and express in your life?

In a moment, I'm going to ask you to write down some of your values, but first I want to explain something that might shift the way you see values and help them be more powerfully in your service, if only by becoming more specific and clear for you.

All of our values matter, even the seemingly superficial ones. However, the real power lies in those values I call "essential."

Essential values are ones that have nothing else inside of them—such as prime numbers, which can't be divided any further. You could call them "source" values. They are really "the heart of the matter."

WHAT QUALITIES DO YOU MOST ADMIRE?

Let's look at money as an example: Suppose you decide that "having money" is a value for you. Fine. Now ask yourself this: "When I have money, what will it bring me?" If you can answer that question with something other than money, then money itself is not an essential value. Look deeper.

You might say money will bring you a house, a new car, travel, education for your kids, or something else. Again, fine. Now, when you have one of those commodities, what will that bring you?

I'm asking you to be a bit more serious and even rigorous about asking these questions. Your answers will probably surprise you—and please you, too.

For instance, if you say you want money so you can have a new house, and then you ask, "If I could have that new house, what would that bring me?" you might answer, "security for my family" or "peace of mind" or "prestige." Now you're getting down to essential stuff, the stuff dreams and success are made of. And the fascinating thing is that money itself is rarely—I'm tempted to say *never*—a truly essential value. Nobody really wants the Midas touch—but many of us *do* want freedom, adventure, fun, recognition, appreciation, belonging, independence, creativity, and so forth.

Be mindful of contribution as a value shared by many leaders. "Speak up for those who cannot speak for themselves, for the rights of all who are destitute" (Proverbs 31:8). Solomon reminds us that contribution is not only financial. Action is as important as helping with money. This is not to say that financial charity is not important. It is. "He who is kind to the poor lends to the Lord, and He will reward him for what he has done" (Proverbs 19:17). We can then call giving "enlightened self-interest." Clearly, contribution must be a value we all share.

Here's what the apostle Paul had to say on the subject: "Therefore, as God's chosen people, holy and dearly loved, clothe yourself with compassion, kindness, humility, gentleness and patience. Bear with each other and forgive whatever grievances you may have against one another" (Colossians 3:12–13). Paul is very clear about what he values and what he expects from others.

Now make a list of the top five values you have in your life, and keep asking yourself clarifying questions until you have no more answers and have gotten down to the essence of each value.

Value 1 _____

Value 2 _____

Value 3 _____

Value 4 _____

Value 5 _____

More often than not, you can't come up with these values by yourself. You may want to do this process with someone else and have him or her ask you questions to flush out the essence of your values.

Plato wrote, "The truth is revealed in dialogue." I believe the truth is revealed through Scripture, prayer, and dialogue. Dialogue is an important element.

My business has me talking to lots of people about their values. I don't ask right out, "So, Joan, what are your essential values?" because most people wouldn't know how to answer that. Instead, I ask about where Joan lives, what she thinks and feels most about, what she'd like to be different in her life, if anything. I ask about her family, her work, her hobbies, and what she does for fun.

Sometimes, if I'm feeling particularly close to the person— and decidedly brave for that moment—I'll ask the most powerful and profound question of all time: "Joan, are you happy?"

Be careful with this one. Some people consider it an intrusion. Others will get so distraught they will "disappear from view," even though they're still sitting right in front of you. It's not a good question to ask at a party, but if you are sincerely interested in that person, and you really want to know what's important to them, *fast*, ask it.

Then listen.

Two things will happen: First, you will learn things about that person that he or she probably hasn't shared with anyone else. You will know them in a way that is actually closer than most of their friends and relatives.

And second, you'll probably make a good friend. Let me tell you a story from Richard Brooke, CEO and President of Oxyfresh USA, that illustrates what I mean.

> A psychologist once did a research project that required he fly from New York to Los Angeles. His task was to sit next to another passenger and engage that person in six hours of conversation, never once making a declarative statement about himself. He was only to ask the other person questions.
>
> When the plane landed, the psychologist had a team of his people there in the airport, ready to interview his fellow

passenger. What they found was that this man, with whom the psychologist had just spent the entire coast-to-coast trip talking, had only two things to say: (1) "That man? The one sitting next to me? Yes—he is the most interesting person I've ever met!" and (2) "His name? Gosh—now that you mention it, I didn't get the fellow's name!"

Ask and you shall receive—all you ever wanted and more. And one of the things you will receive is the key to success in working with other people. Ask them questions that reveal their values—and then listen.

People love to talk about interesting things, and for most of us, the most interesting thing in the world is *ourselves*.

One more thing about values: they change. Just because you've written a list of your top-five values today, doesn't mean you won't have new ones emerge or that the old ones won't be replaced someday—any day.

If there is one law of life I've learned, it's the fact that everything changes. Your beliefs, your values, even your purpose (which we'll talk about next) are ever-changing. That's one way you can tell if you are learning and growing. If you find yourself doing the same-old, same-old for a long time, look out! Change is the way of things in our universe. Everything around us is changing—and you and I must change, too.

Now let's talk about your life purpose.

Life Purpose

I think there are two kinds of people in this world: people who are on-purpose and people who seem rather purposeless. The difference is that one is living his or her life purpose, and the other is not. This is one of those pass-or-fail, black-and-white matters: either you have a purpose that gets you out of bed in the morning, or you don't.

"A man without a purpose," wrote Thomas Carlyle, "is like a ship without a rudder."

Purpose is not something to be completed or finished, like a goal. You achieve your life purpose by living your life in accordance with the values your purpose experiences and expresses.

Purpose is your vision. Purpose calls forth your passion.

Look at people with purpose: Churchill, JFK, Golda Meir, Martin Luther King Jr., Thomas Edison, Michael Jordan, Henry Ford, Margaret Thatcher, Ronald Reagan, Mother Teresa, Babe Ruth . . . The list is endless. From every possible walk of life we acknowledge these heroes and heroines. They are people with purpose.

We recognize public people of purpose easily, from the arts and sciences, sports, politics and leadership, business, government, entertainment, education, and more. But you don't have to be a famous person to live your life in a heroic way. All that's required is having a goal bigger than you are.

And that's the one key I've recognized about purpose: it's always about making a contribution to others.

Look at the list of people above. Every one of those men and women has inspired countless others. No matter how egocentric or self-absorbed any of them may have seemed at any given point in their lives—and it is true that a big sense of self seems to go hand in hand with a big dream—they've all made a difference to people, lots and lots of people. They've had a vision, a goal, a purpose that was bigger than they were at the time—much bigger. That's the key.

We've all heard stories of people whose vision and purpose drove them on to break through seemingly impossible limitations. Purpose is the driving force in all accomplishments of greatness. But such great achievements are not reserved for those public figures who make it onto *The Lifestyles of the Rich and Famous*. In fact, there are many more ordinary people living extraordinary lives than you and I will ever know about.

One thing all of these wonderful people have in common is a clear, powerful life purpose. All they have needed is a stage or a playing field to give them the opportunity to live their lives as the high-achievers their purpose inspires them to be.

None of these people are born with this purpose already in their minds. Now, you can wait around, being as open to the possibilities as possible, and someday I'm sure your life purpose will occur to you. However, if you're excited (as I am!), and you know the awesome power of having a life purpose that brings forth your values and that has you experience the rich rewards life has to offer, you might want to take your imaginative birthright and develop a powerful, passionate purpose right now.

How do you do that?

You go to your heart. Each one of us has been born with gifts written on our heart. Go to your heart, and use your imagination. Remember that the spirit of God can work through your imagination.

Write down your list of values again, followed by a sentence or two that includes a life purpose that would allow you to experience and express those values to the fullest.

Value 1 _____

_____

Value 2 _____

_____

Value 3 _____

_____

Value 4 _____

_____

Value 5 _____

_____

Remember, the key is to contribute to others. I can assure you, if your purpose does not include making a big difference in other people's lives, it's off the mark.

Your life purpose could further be described as the following:

Your life purpose is the cornerstone of your motivation.

Your life purpose is the keystone of your work ethic.

Your life purpose calls forth your passion.

Your life purpose is the standard by which you judge your progress and whether or not you're on- or off-track.

Your life purpose is the BIG DREAM, in which all your other goals and aspirations play supporting parts.

Your life purpose is the reason for your success.

Your life purpose is what gets you out of bed in the morning.

Like a book, a life purpose may not be accurately judged "by its cover." A person's life purpose may be disarmingly simple. In fact, I think the most powerful ones are. Let me show you what I mean.

> YOUR LIFE PURPOSE IS THE BIG DREAM.
>
> ——— ✳ ———

I once had the good fortune to speak with a man who had spent his life working closely with Mother Teresa in her clinic in Calcutta. I was curious about what life purpose lay behind this amazing woman, whose life and work had inspired so many people all around the world. So I asked my new friend, and here's what he told me: "Mother's purpose is to have people die with smiles on their faces."

That's it?! I thought. Here was one of the most awe-inspiring people in the world, a woman devoted to serving humanity, who gave up everything to work with the lowest outcasts and rejected poor of India, and all her purpose amounted to was having people *die smiling?!* It didn't seem right.

So I asked him to tell me more.

He said that in the poverty-stricken streets where Mother Teresa worked her mission, most people died suffering, in agony, abandoned, and alone. That they should die with smiles on their faces, he told me, was the fulfillment of Mother Teresa's work. That's how she knew that through faith and love, she had eased their pain and comforted their lives.

I got it.

Such a simple expression for such a powerful and meaningful purpose.

Service to others is the key to a powerful life purpose. We'll speak more about service in chapter 5, but for now, remember, "The greatest among you will be your servant" (Matthew 23:11). Service brings out the best in all of us—when we are serving others, we really shine. So "let your light shine before men, that they may see your good deeds and praise your Father in heaven" (Matthew 5:16).

Remember, too, that the purpose you're going to write down isn't cast in anything unchangeable. In fact, do it in pencil so you can make all the changes you want, whenever you want.

Go ahead; think about what your heart is telling you and take a crack at writing a rough draft of your life purpose now.

_____

_____

The Purpose of Jesus

Perhaps the most effective way to teach about purpose, or mission, is to see the ultimate example of living for a purpose. Undoubtedly, this is the most important chapter in this book, for we are given a clear example of a purpose-driven life, of *the* purpose-driven life that is the ultimate freedom for those of us who choose to accept it. Let's talk about the ultimate mission—the mission of Jesus.

The main focus of the purpose of Jesus is freedom from sin. All the physical healings that Jesus performed throughout His ministry were physical manifestations of the true healing that occurs inside—forgiveness of sin. Let's speak first about these healings.

In a little town in Galilee, word spread that a healer was coming. Some who heard this had a friend that was paralyzed, and they carried him to see Jesus. The crowd, however, was overwhelming; they couldn't get close to Jesus. But they didn't give up. They hoisted him up on the roof and lowered him through an opening. Their persistence and inventiveness were rewarded. "When Jesus saw their faith, he said, 'Friend, your sins are forgiven' " (Luke 5:20). Not only was the man physically healed, but, more important, he was also spiritually cleansed—his sins were forgiven.

While Jesus was visiting another town in Galilee, a leper threw himself down at Jesus' feet. It's important to understand that leprosy in those days did not simply mean sickness but also isolation, abandonment, and complete exile. Since lepers were disallowed from coming into town, the man must have used his cloak to hide himself. When he threw off his cloak in front of Jesus, everyone backed off—everyone except Jesus. The leper's request was precise: "Lord, if you are willing, you can make me clean" (Luke 5:12). Because the leper knew this was his one chance, you can be sure he prepared his words carefully. He didn't simply want to be healed, but cleansed. He wanted not only his physical health back but also his spiritual health. He wanted to be able to go back to the temple from which he was banned.

At this point, Jesus shocked the crowd. He stretched out his hand to touch the leper and said, "I am willing. . . . Be clean" (Luke 5:13). Much more meaningful than the words was the act of touching the leper. According to Jewish law, when anyone who is ritually unclean, such as a leper, touches someone who is clean, the clean becomes unclean and is banned from the temple. But instead of Jesus becoming unclean, the leper became clean. This was unheard of! Something like this had never happened in the entire Old Testament. Now when unclean and clean met, it was the unclean that was changed. The unclean, and all that this represented—defilement, sin, and death—was forever conquered by Jesus. The leper was freed from his exile and experienced the new exodus that Jesus accomplishes for all of us.

A similar incident occurred when Jesus encountered the woman who had been bleeding for twelve years. Because of the crowd, her fingers barely "touched the edge of his cloak" (Luke 8:44). Immediately she was healed. When Jesus asked who touched Him, the woman was afraid. Again, we need to understand Jewish law to understand her fear. The Torah dictates that a bleeding woman is unclean (Leviticus 15:25). She knew this law. She knew that she would make Jesus unclean by touching Him. But she was desperate. Again, Jesus surprised the crowd. Instead of rebuke, Jesus said, "Daughter, your faith has healed you. Go in peace" (Luke 8:48). Once again, clean overpowered unclean and exile became exodus.

This theme of exodus is vital in the purpose of Jesus. When Peter, James, and John saw Jesus on Mount Tabor speaking with Moses and Elijah, only Luke shared their topic of conversation: "They spoke about his departure, which he was about to bring to fulfillment at Jerusalem" (Luke 9:31). Another word for departure is *exodus*. Who better for Jesus to discuss His exodus with than Moses, the leader of the first Exodus?

Just like the first Exodus, the new exodus requires a Passover meal. The Jewish holiday of Passover celebrates the Exodus from Egypt. It is often called the Holiday of Freedom. This time, the Passover meal ushers in the new exodus—not freedom from slavery, but freedom from sin. This, of course, is the very essence of the purpose of Jesus.

Jesus had a purpose and He fulfilled that purpose.

What is your purpose? I want you to understand the power of a purpose-driven life. Your purpose comes first. All else follows.

Once you've established your life purpose, all the other success secrets we're going to explore in this book become easy.

But if all of this business of positive beliefs, living your values, and developing a life purpose is simply a matter of *making it up*, why haven't most people already made it all up in a way that works for them?

The answer is *fear*.

SECRET 4

Fear is what each of us must learn to conquer

Secret #4

Fearlessness

> "When you lie down, you will not be afraid; when you lie down, your sleep will be sweet."
>
> PROVERBS 3:24

F ear. An interesting subject to tackle head on, but an easy one to overcome. To get a handle on fear, let's return for a moment to the matter of belief.

Remember that belief is the key to success. No matter what career or business enterprise you choose, you must believe in what you are doing. You must believe in your company, their mission, integrity, and what they stand for, and you must believe in the people you work with, as well.

There's no way to fake any of this. If you don't believe in what you're doing, you simply cannot be successful.

We've all met business people whose words just didn't ring true, like a Honda salesperson who drives a Toyota. How many people do you know who are trading their time for money in a job they can't stand? How persuasive, honest, and service-oriented is a person who doesn't believe in what he or she is doing for work—much less *to make a living?*

Belief, like life purpose, is one of those pass-or-fail things. You either have it or you don't. And, of course, one of the most important beliefs of all is: *You must believe in who God made you to be.*

You must believe in your values, your unique talents and special gifts, your purpose, your goals, dreams, and aspirations. You must KNOW that what you are doing is making a difference; that you and your efforts are a real contribution to others. After all, if you don't believe in who God made you to be and in what you're doing—who will?

Everything Is Sales

The key to successful sales and selling is belief. Every business, career, occupation, enterprise of any kind, is *sales.* In fact, every interaction you have with all of the people you come in contact with each day is sales.

I know a lot of people don't want to hear that *everything* is sales. That's because most people are in the habit of saying (or thinking), "I *can't* sell," "I *don't like* to sell or to be sold anything," and "I *won't* sell." (How's that for no possibility?)

I suppose that's why we pay salespeople so much. They're the Green Berets of business: "It's a dirty job—but *somebody's* got to do it." And since nobody else wants to sell, it's obviously one of the most dangerous and risky jobs around, so those high-income-earning salespeople must be getting hazard pay!

Just for fun, next time you meet someone who says he doesn't like or want to sell, ask him to tell you more about that. Then sit back and listen as he spends the next five minutes or more masterfully *selling you* on how he *can't sell.*

The truth is, everything is sales.

We sell our friends on going with us to the movie we want to see, the restaurant where we want to eat, the dessert we want to share. We sell our kids on believing in themselves—and on cleaning up their rooms. We sell ideas, concepts, thoughts, opinions, and feelings. Teachers sell knowledge and discovery.

The most important sale of the day is what we sell to ourselves.

When people say they can't sell, it's simply not the truth. What they are really saying is "I don't *believe* I can sell. I don't *believe* in myself." And do you know what? That's not true, either! They believe, all right. They have a *negative belief* about sales. They have a *negative belief* about themselves. And every negative belief, no matter how artfully conceived or rationally explained, comes down to being one big, near-universal negative belief that every single person on the planet shares—FEAR.

Fear: Friend or Foe?

The enemy of a powerful belief is fear. Fear is what hurts us, stops us in the successful pursuit of our goals and purpose. And fear is what each of us must learn to conquer.

I know there are schools of philosophy that say, "Love your fears." That doesn't make much sense to me. We all have fear. Some of it's healthy, too. But love it? I'd rather lose it.

Now, let's make a distinction here. I'm glad I have some fears (or better said, some fears have me), such as being afraid of stepping in front of a speeding truck. I'm afraid of things like chain saws and other power tools, guns, cars going 120 mph, 220 volts of electricity, tornadoes, drunk drivers, war in the Middle East, and other things like that. I consider these to be pretty healthy fears. They compel me to act with great respect and take care when crossing the street, sawing logs, or repairing an appliance. Those fears motivate me to take positive action. It would be foolish to be fearless in those and many other situations.

I've got another fear: that we'll waste our planet's resources and regret our behavior for generations to come. I consider that a healthy fear. It leads me to recycle and use durable things that last, to buy products from "green" companies and people who've made a commitment to a cleaner, healthier, more respectful world. That's another example of a fear that serves me.

What examples do you have of fears that strengthen you, keep you aware, fears that support you in your life and work?

My point is that fear in itself isn't good or bad. Just like beliefs, fear can be either healthy or unhealthy. Fear is a tool, and like any tool that can be used to build or to destroy, the quality of how it serves you or undermines your efforts is up to you. It's just another choice.

In most situations (other than the crossing-the-freeway, re-wiring-your-home, life-threatening ones), choosing fear means choosing a life of unfulfilled goals and aspirations. This choice is the true enemy of success.

Fear of What?

The most common fear we human beings have is fear of the unknown. For some reason, we got it into our collective minds ages ago that we had to know what would happen before we could take action. "Safety first" was drummed into us until it became "fear of the unknown." While this is the most common fear of all—probably the source of that other "monster fear," fear of dying—the following story may serve to rid you of this fear once and for all.

A man was convicted of treason and sentenced to death by firing squad. As the drums rolled, the man faced his executioners. The commanding general announced, "Sir, you have a choice: you can accept your fate and die before this firing squad, or you can go through that black door over there."

He was given two hours to think about it.

Two hours later, the man was returned to the prison yard, placed in front of the firing squad, his hands bound, a blindfold covering his eyes. The general then asked him, "What have you chosen?"

The man replied, "I have no idea what I might face behind that black door. It could be a most terrible fate—I choose the firing squad."

The order was given, shots rang out. The man fell to the ground dead.

As they were leaving the prison, an aide turned to the general and asked, "Sir, what was behind that door?"

Without expression, the general replied, "Freedom."

Risky Business

Fear of the unknown comes from the desire to avoid risk. Very often, risk means anxiety. Did you know that the character in Chinese that represents the concept "crisis" is made up of two smaller characters? One means "risk" and the other means "opportunity." To reduce anxiety, people avoid the unknown.

Facing the unknown means accepting the challenge of the unknown, and to accept that challenge, we must have self-discipline and belief in who God made us to be.

Have you ever seen a James Bond movie? Secret Agent 007 has this tendency to walk right into his enemy's stronghold and confront the sinister villain (Goldfinger, Dr. No, and the others) face-to-face. I love it! Bond has no idea what's going to happen, but you can be sure that if he messes up, it's going to be *horrible*. One time he was going to be fed to the sharks. Another time, cut in half with a laser. But no matter—he always gets out of it. He keeps his cool. He is disciplined. He believes in himself—even when he has no idea what's coming next.

For too many people, self-discipline literally means self-punishment. What do we do with an out-of-control twelve-year-old boy headed for what used to be called juvenile delinquency? We send him to military school. Why? Discipline—and that's punishment.

Discipline, however, comes from the word "disciple," which means two very interesting things: *to follow* and *learner*. "Whoever loves discipline loves knowledge, but he who hates correction is stupid" (Proverbs 12:1). Discipline comes from following and learning from someone or something. *Self-discipline* comes from learning about and following *one's own beliefs*.

People who follow their limiting beliefs by avoiding learning about the unknown are actually very disciplined. They never take chances. You see, discipline, too, is either strengthening or limiting. When following a positive belief and purpose, discipline is actually a freeing and powerful concept, not a limiting one.

Discipline is something we can all cultivate. A good synonym for discipline is *integrity*. It's as simple as doing what you say you're going to do—keeping your word. And you can do that, especially with yourself, only when your belief is bigger than your fears.

There's another aspect of fear of the unknown that most people don't consider, and that's the fear of simply *looking at things differently*. We get so stuck in what we think we know and the sameness of things, yet the safety of that prevents us from even considering something new. It's a security that prohibits us from looking out beyond that old tried-and-true position or point of view. And that's a major stumbling block to coming up with new and better ways of doing things.

Live and work like an artist with a blank canvas. Be willing to risk the inevitable "failures" that going beyond your experience presents. That's where all the real rewards are. After all, if you keep doing things the way you've been doing them, you're bound to end up with what you've already got.

The reason most people aren't willing to do this is a *fear of failure*.

"To Fail or Not to Fail"—What a Question!

The next fear to conquer is the fear of failure. And the surest way to do that is to change your understanding of the value of what we usually call "failure."

One of America's true high-achievers, Thomas Edison, had this to say about "failure": "To double your success rate, you must double your failure rate."

Zig Ziglar has said that if you only close one out of twenty-five sales calls, each failure is simply one step closer to making that next sale!

Do you know that failures are critical to success? There is not a "successful" man or woman on this earth who was not a major failure many times before attaining that mantle of success.

A very wealthy businessman once began a speech by saying, "It's true that I am successful, probably the most successful person in this room. Would you like to know why? It is because I have failed more times than anyone here."

Check out the impressive track record of another famous success story:

Fired from his job in '32.
Defeated for legislature in '32.
Declared bankruptcy in '33.
Elected to legislature in '34.
Sweetheart died in '35.
Had a nervous breakdown in '36.
Defeated for Speaker in '38.
Defeated in nomination for Congress in '43.
Elected to Congress in '46.
Lost bid for renomination in '48.
Rejected for Land Officer in '49.
Defeated for Senate in '54.
Defeated for nomination for Vice President in '56.
Defeated for Senate a second time in '58.
And in 1860, Abraham Lincoln was elected
President of the United States of America.

Name the two greatest home-run hitters in the history of baseball. Babe Ruth and Hank Aaron.

Can you name the two players who had the greatest number of strikeouts? Babe Ruth and Hank Aaron.

Do you see what the wealthy businessman is saying?

Thomas Edison had a dream of making a working electric incandescent light bulb. Yet time after time his experiments failed. After about the one-hundredth time, one of his frustrated young associates said to him, "Can't you see that this isn't destined to work, that you're not going to succeed? You've failed one hundred times already!"

Edison replied, "I have not failed at all, I have successfully determined one hundred ways that it will not work; therefore, I'm one hundred ways closer to the one way it will work."

This brings us to a point that is often overlooked. Those around us may do their best to keep us in fear and keep us discouraged. When the Israelites attempted to rebuild the temple during their first exile, "The people around them set out to discourage the people of Judah and make them afraid to go on building" (Ezra 4:4). The reality is that not that much has changed since biblical times. We need to remember that it is our choice to accept or reject the discouragement of others.

Failure and success are just two more things we make up. To Edison's assistant, the great inventor had failed a hundred times. But to Edison himself, he succeeded a hundred times in learning what *not* to do.

Is it helpful for you to define or describe yourself as a failure? Perhaps you think if you fail often enough, you'll get to a point where you just can't stand it anymore, and you'll start succeeding. That's called *backward motivation*. Well, why not start right now by acknowledging your successes instead?

Here's a great exercise: I'm going to ask you to list ten successes you've had today in the spaces provided below. Even if you're reading this just after you've awakened early in the morning, and you don't think you've done anything successful yet, I want you to list ten successes you've already had today:

1. _____

2. _____

3. _____

4. _____

5. _____

6. _____

7. _____

8. _____

9. _____

10. _____

How did you do? Did you have trouble listing ten successes? If you did, that's a clue that the way you define things is not serving you, not encouraging you. You still think it works to pile up failures until there's no more room for them and you'll just *have* to succeed.

Did you get out of bed this morning? *That's a success.* Did you shower, or shave, or brush your teeth? Did you pray? *Those are successes.* What else did you do today? *That's a success . . . that's a success . . . that's a success!*

You *must* get into the habit of defining your actions and the results that occur in your life and work as successful. And honestly, that's all success is. It's a habit. And like any other habit you have, you learn the habit by repetition. You do it over, and over, and over, and over . . . until it's something you do without thinking.

You made a habit of tying your shoes. You don't think about *how* you do it anymore. You just do it. At first, you had to do that whole "rabbit runs around the tree and down through the hole" business, but after a while, tying your shoes stopped being a rabbit and started being a habit. No thought. You just do it.

Success (or failure) is just the same. If you set a task for yourself that each and every evening before you go to sleep you will list (in writing) ten successes—or twenty-five or fifty, if you're impatient and want the crash course—then very soon, you will establish the habit of success.

Can you imagine a better habit to have? I guarantee you can do this. It's easy and fun—and, it works!

The Success Habitude

We call these ingrained, habitual attitudes "habitudes." And this is the habitude you need to have if you want to avoid failure, disappointment, poverty, and loneliness.

By the way, I want to stress that, to me, failure and poverty do not mean the same thing. For the sake of this book, I'm assuming that most people desire financial success along with all the other successes of a richly rewarding life. After all, in this Western culture of ours, you're going to require money to achieve many of the goals you've set for yourself. And in a very real sense, money is required for freedom in today's world. But there are many poor people who are not failures—and many rich ones who are!

However, the *fear* of poverty has the same root as the fear of failure.

Poverty and wealth are diametrically opposed. If you don't want poverty, you simply must stay away from it—on all levels, not just financial.

There's emotional poverty, social poverty, intellectual poverty, and more, just as there is abundance in all these areas. Avoiding these poverties may sound difficult to do, but as I said earlier, one of the few things over which you have true and total control is your thought life—and remember, your thoughts will become your reality. After all, "Who of you by worrying can add a single hour to his life?" (Matthew 6:27). Yet by that same worrying, we can certainly take many hours away from our lives.

Your thoughts are something you can choose. In fact, it's with our thoughts that we have the God-given power of choice. Once again, you must have the discipline and the focus to keep all of your positive thoughts in your mind while removing all negative thoughts.

Have you ever tried to kick out a negative thought? (There's that "try" again! The word itself is a clue that you're on the wrong track!) It's like taking in a stray animal, feeding it for a couple of weeks, and then deciding you don't want it around anymore. It just keeps coming back again and again. It's not easy to get rid of negative thoughts, no matter how unwanted they may be. In fact, lots of times it's nearly *impossible*. That's why so many people pay such good money for courses and products to help them *try* to stop smoking, lose weight, and get rid of any other prevalent bad habit.

THE EMOTIONAL ENERGY OF FEELING IS A POWERFUL ALLY.

———✳———

Instead, what you do is simply replace that limiting thought with a positive one. Each time that limiting thought or fear starts to replay in your mind, stop the thought mid-sentence, and replace it with its opposite—with a positive thought.

Remember, your thoughts often become your reality. Your thoughts determine your feelings, and the emotional energy of feeling is a powerful ally for shaping either success or failure. Again, it's a choice and it's up to each of us, moment by moment, to make the choice for life and success.

And that's another important point: this business of developing positive thoughts is a moment-by-moment thing. The instant you succeed in turning a negative to a positive, that negative is going to do its best to reassert itself. After all, it's fighting for its life! But then, so are you—and it is really all up to you which of the two wins.

What State Do You Live In?

No, that's not an inquiry about your geographical location. What is *your state of mind?*

All fears, including those most destructive fears of poverty and failure, are nothing more than states of mind.

States of mind come about by the mental habits we choose over and over until they exist automatically. When you or I are in a given state of mind, we've probably just found ourselves there without really knowing how we got there or why. We don't plan the trip. We just show up in Doubtville or Can't City or wherever.

This is important, because these states of mind can *cause our results*. And they absolutely can cause the most negative and most disastrous results. So developing those states of mind that serve and give power to your goals and purpose is a very important skill to learn. And yes, it takes discipline: learning and following our positive beliefs.

Fortunately, there is a wonderful built-in mechanism that will help you tremendously: *The conscious mind can hold only one thought at a time.* This is a real blessing. It makes it so much easier to remove a negative thought if you can replace it immediately with a positive thought.

How do you do that?

Do you remember when Julie Andrews sang "My Favorite Things" in *The Sound of Music*? Whether it's raindrops on roses, or Christmas, or ice cream, or the car you dream of having, college for your kids, the freedom to paint or dance—whatever it is for you, that's what you can use to replace any and all negative thoughts.

See yourself doing what you've always wanted to do. In your mind, picture yourself having achieved your dreams and desires: driving that car, sailing that ocean, speaking to eight hundred people and inspiring them all. The minute a negative thought pops into mind, slap the success video of your life into the VCR of your mind. And keep running it again and again, until it's the state of mind you normally walk around in.

Now you're living in a great state!

One of the first things I learned to do to shift my state of mind was the exercise of tallying up each day's successes. Soon not only was I increasing my habit of success but another thing I didn't expect also began to happen:

I began to realize how grateful I was.

Really, I began building the *habit of gratitude* as well as the habit of success. And believe me, if you want to walk around in a powerful state of mind that will have you on top of the world, bringing you great results you never dreamed were possible—gratitude is it.

As I wrote early in this book, I believe that had I simply been more grateful to God for what He had given me, I could have avoided much of my troubles. "This is the day the Lord has made; let us rejoice and be glad in it" (Psalm 118:24). This psalm specifically teaches us the habit of gratitude. The amazing thing is, Jesus recited this psalm the night before He was crucified, knowing full well it was His Last Supper. Psalm 118 is part of the traditional Passover liturgy, and Jesus, fully aware of the painful death that awaited Him in mere hours, recited this psalm with an attitude of thanksgiving.

In Judaism, the rabbis have written blessings of thanksgiving that surround every aspect of an individual's life. This comes from the basic belief in the truth of Genesis—that God made the world and it was good. The Orthodox Jew begins each day by reciting the "Modeh Ani" prayer: "Thank you, living, eternal King; for in Your mercy You have restored my soul to me. Great is Your trustworthiness." Jesus teaches just how thankful we need to be!

I regularly replace a negative state of mind with a grateful state of mind simply by listing all the things in my life that I'm grateful for. I start saying them to myself one by one: I'm thankful for my relationship with Jesus . . . my wonderful family . . . my many new friends (and I list them each by name). I can go on forever. The sun, this day, the clouds, the rain, the flowers, my car, the speedometer, numbers, lights, windshields—see how the list of things you're grateful for just builds and grows? And the result? Instant smiles! A great state of mind. It's so powerful!

Fear carries with it the danger of paralyzing you and completely stifling your actions; and even more important, fear kills inspiration and imagination. *Fears* of failure obviously lead to *beliefs* of failure; fears of poverty lead to beliefs of poverty. Fears encourage procrastination, kill ambition, and invite unhappiness in every form. I'm convinced that many illnesses, even organic disorders, can be reversed into health by replacing the limiting fears in our minds with powerful beliefs. "The prayer offered in faith will make the sick person well" (James 5:15). As we said earlier, faith is the most powerful belief of all.

The way to conquer fear is to strongly insist that it leave. Remember, the subconscious mind will believe anything you tell it. Develop states of mind that support and encourage you.

The Critic

There's one last fear we need to discuss: the fear of criticism.

This fear is commonly called the fear of "what others think of me." I call it "the fear of not looking good."

How we look to others is one of the most powerful motivators of human behavior. Now, please understand, it's not that there's anything wrong with looking good. I like to look good. I'm sure you do, too. But when we sacrifice our integrity to look good, when we lie—by commission or omission—to protect our public image, we undermine our goals and purpose and we champion beliefs of fear and failure.

Shakespeare had this fear—and its antidote—pegged perfectly when he said, "This above all: To thine own self be true."

I want to point out that the number one reason people try to steal our dreams—and that's what a great deal of criticism comes down to—is that our dreams force other people to take responsibility for themselves.

Our dreams literally compel other people to admit to themselves that they, too, are in control of their own lives. Our dreams force others to take responsibility for where they are today and where they will be tomorrow.

Fear is contagious, and people want you to catch it. The Israelites knew this and took precautions. Before battle, the officers spoke: "Is any man afraid or fainthearted? Let him go home so that his brothers will not become disheartened too" (Deuteronomy 20:8). We cannot allow other people's fears to frighten us.

When you take a stand, you're going to catch some flak from those people who haven't the courage you do. It comes with the territory. *Courage*, by the way, means "heart" and "being on purpose." And I want you to know that I know that all the changes we are talking about here require courage. The true warrior is one who has the courage to do battle with the enemies within himself.

Speaking of courage, which comes first: having courage and then taking action, or taking action and then drawing courage from it?

I'll let Henry Ford answer this one: "Courage follows action."

Don't be surprised at people's desperate fear of criticism. After all, for many centuries human beings have been punished, even killed, for having the courage to express beliefs that were different from those held by the majority: Galileo, Joan of Arc, Martin Luther King Jr., and many more. We have a horrible intolerance for new and different beliefs that threaten the status quo.

Nonetheless, we must resist this fear with all our might. The fear of criticism leads to indecision, and it is the primary reason for lack of ambition, motivation, and purpose.

President Theodore Roosevelt said,

COURAGE FOLLOWS ACTION.

> It is not the critic who counts—not the man who points out how the strong man stumbled, or where the doer could have done better. The credit belongs to the man who is actually in the arena, whose face is marred by dust and sweat and blood. Who strives valiantly, who errs and comes short again and again, who knows the great enthusiasms, the great devotions, and spends himself in a worthy cause. . . . Who, at the least, knows in the end the triumph of high achievement, and who, at the worst, if he fails, at least fails while doing greatly, so that his place shall never be with those cold and timid souls who know neither victory nor defeat.

We can be thankful together for the fact that we have the power to overcome and conquer the fear of criticism and all other fears.

It's fun for me to be a warrior in this battle with my fears. At first, I wasn't very good at it, and just as in sports or any other pursuit, I have the most fun when I'm good at something. But I was surprised at how good I became, how quickly. It doesn't take long.

I also like a challenge. Once I got good at fighting fear, do you know what happened? I started looking for bigger ones to battle. That's the one problem with this business of conquering fear: once you do it, there are very few fears around to fight anymore! Why? "By standing firm you will gain life" (Luke 21:19). Literally. Everything we desire is available to us.

And do you know what that means? It means we need to move on to still more exciting challenges—and even more fulfilling ones.

SECRET 5

When we master our attitude, we master our life

Secret #5

Attitude

> "Do not be anxious about anything, but in everything, by prayer and petition, with thanksgiving, present your requests to God."
>
> PHILIPPIANS 4:6

A ttitude is the switch that turns on everything else! When you master your attitude, you master your life. It's been said that any fact facing us is not as important as our attitude toward it, for that determines our success or failure.

Before anybody buys anything from you—a product, an invitation, a recommendation, an opportunity, a possibility, *anything*—they first must buy *your attitude*. The quality and effectiveness of all your communications is a matter of attitude. The attitude you have while you're with other people is the greatest influence on their thoughts and feelings. Your attitude means much more to people than what you say to them.

Have you ever heard it said, "People don't care how much you know, until they know how much you care"? That's attitude—and that's power.

ATTITUDE IS THE SWITCH THAT TURNS ON EVERYTHING ELSE!

Do this: Have a conversation with somebody you know well (choose a friend so as not to offend), and while you're speaking to them, keep telling yourself you don't care about them. Just keep saying in your head, "I don't care. I don't care. I don't care," and watch what happens. I'm certain you can imagine the outcome.

One of my goals is to have every person I speak with successfully cultivate an attitude of PASSION. I am convinced that an attitude of passion inspires peak performance. My recorded voicemail greeting message ends with the words "Have a great day—and *live with passion.*"

Mastering Your Attitude

When I use the word *mastering* in this context, it means to rule and have authority over your attitude. I am convinced that one of the most powerful keys to success is directing and managing your attitude. Every high-achieving leader is more than adept at this skill—please understand that it is a *skill* and therefore can be learned, as is true of any other craft or skill.

Every dynamic leader I've met is a master of his or her attitude. In fact, we could probably separate people into two broad categories: those who are masters of their attitude and those who are servants of theirs.

How do you become the master of your attitude? How do you stay "up," especially during those tough times when the chips are down?

The answer is surprisingly simple. (And isn't that a joy!)

Super-successful people continuously run their own highlight films in the movie screens of their minds.

You've seen those short clips of spectacular athletic plays on the sports section of the evening news. That's what I mean. Successful people are always watching themselves make that diving catch, that spinning basket, that world-breaking effort that results in a big, BIG WIN! They just change the game to fit their own circumstances.

When the going gets tough, the tough watch movies of themselves in positive, productive action. Another way of saying this is: Successful people believe their own press.

I know, I know—we were taught not to do that. It's self-centered and ego-stroking, right? Not necessarily. Remember that your own success is the greatest gift you have to give to those whose lives you touch. You know the expression "When you laugh, the whole world laughs with you—but when you cry, you cry alone." Here's another way of seeing that: "When you succeed, the whole world succeeds with you—but when you simply TRY, you try alone!"

Your success is a gift. The truth is, cultivating a success habitude in yourself is the opposite of being egocentric. To be self-centered is to wallow in self-pity and mediocrity, to shirk from stepping up to the plate to swing the full home-run successes of which you're capable. "A cheerful heart is good medicine, but a crushed spirit dries up the bones" (Proverbs 17:22).

So go ahead—get your high-performance movies ready to play in your mind's screening room!

Now, these highlight films of you in action can come from

your own actual experience, or you can make them up. If you don't have stored away some stock footage of you doing the fantastic in a similar situation, use your imagination to make up a new one. Either way, they're both *real* in terms of how your mind perceives them.

This highlight film of yours will produce an immediate positive result—a *positive attitude.* Seeing yourself at your best is the best way to shift your attitude into high (performance) gear.

Now you know that part of my vision is to instill *passion* in people. I *intend* and *expect* to persuade every one of you reading these words to demand more from life, to never again settle for less than the very best your life has to offer. After all, I reason, if we are made in God's image and likeness—and I *absolutely believe we are*—then how could we possibly accept mediocrity?

We can't. You shouldn't. And *you won't!*

If I approached writing this book with an attitude of "Don't worry, be happy," you'd probably respond to it with a "Thanks a lot, but . . ." From reading what you have so far, you know I feel much more passionately than that. I know you are—we all are—designed for success. So expect success! You deserve it. It's coming right at you, right now. That's the attitude I'm writing with, and that's how I know this book is destined to encourage and inspire millions of people.

And what's more, that's the attitude I ask you to *read* these pages with.

The Questions of Attitude

One of the most powerful ways to maintain a powerful attitude is to ask yourself powerful questions.

It is the kinds of questions you ask yourself that determine your focus and direct your actions. There are three questions I've found that are exceptionally powerful in generating and maintaining a positive, passionate attitude. Here they are:

Powerful Question #1: What's Great About This?

No matter what the conditions around you, you *can always* find an answer to this question. I know it may be difficult at first. But really, all you need is practice.

Once I had to be in San Francisco for a breakfast presentation to two hundred representatives of Primerica Financial Services at seven that morning. The meeting was two and a half hours away from where I was staying at the time. So up and off I go, arriving at the same time the sun came up—and there were twelve people in the room.

Not two hundred. Twelve.

Okay, I said to myself, *what's great about this?* And my self began to grumble, "Well, up at four in the morning—pitch black, cold, damp—I drive two and a half hours. I expect two hundred people, and there are only twelve! *Grumble, grumble . . .* Hey! There is *nothing* great about this!"

I knew from experience what this really meant. It meant that I had to ask the question again in a way that would get my attention. So I screamed it—inside my head, of course.

And then I realized that what was so great was the opportunity I had to inspire a dozen people to break through to new levels of passion, happiness, and success—which I would have slept through if I wasn't there.

I had my answer, but then an interesting thing happened— and it happens ninety-nine times out of a hundred when I ask myself this question. The what's-great-about-this? answers *kept coming.*

Having only twelve people enabled me to be much more

intimate with each person in the group. I could give each person personal attention, and we could all take more time on the points of my presentation, which would involve them all more, and make us more powerful as a group, because the quality of our relationships would raise the level of the work we were doing together two or three times what it would have been if the group were larger . . . and we would be able to go deeper and higher, and the people would be able to interact more with me and among themselves, which always supercharges the group and results in building them together as a team . . . and I knew when that happened they would go back to their friends and families inspired and charged up, and that would cause a daisy-chain effect that would spread the word out in a geometric way and eventually touch hundreds, even thousands of people, when all I did was meet with twelve, and WOW!

You get the idea.

The what's-great-about-this? question almost always results in an attitude of gratitude as a *fringe benefit!* It simply comes free with the asking of the question. It's not even about having the "right" answer!

Next question:

Powerful Question #2: What Can I Learn From This?

When we stop learning, our minds turn to mush. Why? Because the mind is the strongest muscle of all, and the old physical fitness slogan is true for mental muscle tone, too: *Use it or lose it!* When the government filed its lawsuit against me, and depression hit, I refused growth of any kind. I wouldn't pick up a book; I wouldn't engage in any meaningful conversation; I wouldn't even consider seeing what the Bible had to say to me. I simply stopped learning, and decay began to set in. Soon my thinking slowed, and everything else followed.

"Stop listening to instruction, my son, and you will stray from the words of knowledge" (Proverbs 19:27). This can't be a halfway, maybe, sort-of thing. Learning must never, ever stop. You can afford to skip a meal, but don't skip reading a book, because the information you don't get CAN hurt you!

A commitment at the level of complete devotion to lifelong learning is something I've discovered every high-achiever shares. Asking this question often makes modeling that powerful success principle effortless and automatic.

Powerful Question #3: What Needs to Change to Make It Happen?

There is always an *it*—the envisioned result, and a *change* that's required to bring *it* into being. It's another common characteristic of high-achievers. They're not only flexible, they have a love affair going on with change. They have a *passion* for change. Not just external change but internal change. All high-achievers understand that changing things within you comes before changing things around you.

And so it is for high-achievers in any field of enterprise or endeavor. They ride the waves of change like an expert surfer— like a dolphin.

High-achievers realize that there is "a time to tear down and a time to build" (Ecclesiastes 3:3); they realize that the seasons change. People who are passionate about their living and working, *love* change—as well they should, for it is the one and only absolute in this relative world of ours. Things will change. You can count on it.

"What needs to change to make it happen?" is one constant question in the background for all people of passion. It keeps them open, up, curious, innovative, and very productive.

One final point before we move on—it is true of all the high-achievers I've studied: they believe *the best is yet to come.*

The Servant Attitude

To inspire your success, you must develop an attitude about who you are that *serves you*; an attitude that strengthens your purpose, that sets the stage for the full expression of your values, that fuels your beliefs and supports you in conquering your fears and accomplishing your goals and aspirations. For many people, the attitude that serves them best includes serving others.

I was flying one day from Sacramento, California to Fort Lauderdale, Florida. The flight took off at 9:00 A.M. from California, and by 9:20 the man in the seat next to me was on his second Bloody Mary! It looked like it was going to be an interesting trip.

When we arrived in Florida, my seatmate was, to say the least, sloshed. I was in Good Samaritan mode, so I helped navigate him off the plane down to baggage claim, where we soon discovered that his bags were not to be found. I escorted this fellow over to lost baggage, where he promptly went ballistic, heaping loud, slurred verbal abuse on the airline attendant.

She was a saint. Calm and composed, she listened intently, nodding her head and apologizing to this angry, obnoxious, drunken passenger.

When my seatmate walked away to gain strength for another assault, I said to the woman, "How do you deal with people like this all the time?"

She replied, "He's right. We shouldn't have lost his bags. And besides, see the sign?" She pointed above our heads. "It says

LOST BAGS. People don't come to me to thank us for their luggage having arrived safely!"

The man returned and started in on her again. She calmly reached out her hand and put it on his arm, said gently, yet with amazing strength, "Sir, currently there are two people in the world who care about your lost bags—and one of them is rapidly losing interest."

She was incredible.

She finally located his bags, informed him they were on a flight that would arrive in an hour, took all his information down, and promised his luggage would be delivered the moment it arrived. She would see to it personally.

I poured my friend into a cab, and then I went back into the airport terminal to tell that woman what a contribution she had made. Then I told her what a difference she had made to me personally as a stand for the power of attitude. She was a living example of servant leadership. I've never forgotten her.

We have all been given certain gifts by our Father. "Each one should use whatever gift he has received to serve others" (1 Peter 4:10). Service needs to become a way of life for us. When Jesus said, "The greatest among you will be your servant" (Matthew 23:11) He meant it, and He lived it completely. Aside from the ultimate sacrifice and service He made for us—dying on the cross so that we might live—His whole life while on earth personified service. During the Last Supper, Jesus "poured water into a basin and began to wash his disciples' feet" (John 13:5). Can you imagine? Remember these three words: service, service, service!

It's not the circumstances of our lives that determine our success, it's how we react and respond to those situations. And the *how* of that is our attitude. Stanley Judd said it perfectly:

You may be dead broke, and that's a reality, but in spirit you may be brimming over with optimism, joy, and energy. The reality of life may result from many outside factors, none of which you can control. Your attitudes, however, reflect the ways in which you evaluate what is happening.

What kind of attitude do you need to cultivate to generate success? There are all kinds of powerful attitudes. I mentioned one at the end of the previous chapter that has served me greatly—an attitude of gratitude. An "up" attitude is another. A million-dollar attitude is yet another.

There's a wonderful story about three bricklayers at a new building site:

A visitor walks over to the first bricklayer and asks, "What are you doing?" The first worker looks up from his bricks and says, "What does it look like I'm doing? I'm laying bricks, you idiot!"

The man walks over to the second worker and asks again, "What are you doing?" The bricklayer looks over at him, slightly annoyed, and replies, "Can't you see, I'm building a wall."

Finally, he approaches the third bricklayer and asks for the third time, "What are you doing?" The third bricklayer sits back, looks up at him, and says, "I'm building a hospital for sick kids, so they can come here for help and get cured."

That's the kind of attitude you're looking for. Why? "A happy heart makes the face cheerful, but heartache crushes the spirit" (Proverbs 15:13). We all know that is true from our personal experiences. Heartache does crush the spirit, and then the body follows.

John Wooden, another legendary coach and master of successful living, puts it this way: "Things turn out best for the people who make the best of how things turn out."

That's all positive thinking is: having a positive attitude.

The Victim Dictum

You can't let others determine your attitude. Before I realized this principle, I was one of the world's biggest victims. Even little things could incite me to anger or despair.

I remember driving down the parkway one day when a car from three lanes over on the left swerved across all the traffic and cut me off to exit. For hours afterward I was railing and grumbling about the jerk who'd cut me off to everybody who would listen (and even those who wouldn't). Naturally, I got very little accomplished that day. Of course, that man, if he ever realized anything was wrong at all, probably forgot about me as soon as he exited the parkway. Why on earth should I have allowed that character to affect my attitude for the whole day?

I have learned the strength and the power in these three words: LET IT GO! Now I realize no one can harm me, bother me, or perturb me, unless I accept the hurt. No one can inconvenience you unless you acknowledge that you were inconvenienced. Eleanor Roosevelt said it this way: "No one can make you feel inferior without your consent."

All of the hurt, anger, disappointment, frustration, and other negative thoughts and feelings we blame on other people are simply *not the truth.* They all exist only in our own minds. We make them up. It's a matter of *our* attitude.

Motivational teacher and author Zig Ziglar tells a story of being in a Kansas City airport, tired, beat, and anxious to get home—when he learned his flight had been canceled.

"Fantastic!" Ziglar exclaimed.

The harried ticket agent looked as if Zig were the strangest thing she'd ever seen in her life, and said, "Sir, I just told you your flight was cancelled, and you replied, 'Fantastic.' Why is that so fantastic?"

"Well," Ziglar said, "there must be a good reason to cancel the flight. It could be bad weather or a mechanical problem, and either way I think it's great that you and your people are looking out for my welfare and keeping me safe."

"I'm afraid the next flight I can get you on won't be for a number of hours," the agent said.

"Fantastic!" Ziglar replied.

Again, the incredulous agent asked, "And why is *that* fantastic?"

"Well, this is the first time I've ever been in this nice new airport. It's cold and wintry outside, but warm and comfortable in here. There's a great-looking coffee shop over there, and I've got a lot of reading and writing to catch up on, so I'll just take advantage of the free office and get all my work done!"

"Fantastic!" the ticket agent said with a smile.

"You bet!" Ziglar smiled back and went off to work in his "free office" with the convenient catering service.

Of course, Zig could have huffed and puffed, gotten bent all out of shape, and tried to bend everybody else, too—but the plane *still* wouldn't have left for hours. Either way, the facts of the trip would not have changed—but the *experience* was totally transformed.

Positive attitudes influence positive results. Remember, before people buy anything you're offering, they buy your attitude—no matter what you're selling.

I'm tempted to go into a lengthy sermon on sowing and reaping at this point, but I'll hold that for another book. For now, simply understand the scriptural truth that you will, in fact, reap what you sow. That's just the way it is. The process doesn't start with reaping; it starts with sowing. If you really need to reap, then you really need to sow. And the place to start is with your attitude.

My mission is to have millions of readers turn their hearts to Jesus Christ. I'm jump-out-of-my-seat excited about that, and I expect it to happen. Because of this, I wouldn't dare write a single word of this book without first praying and asking God to help me—not only with my words but also with my attitude.

Reinventing the Past

We choose our thoughts, and our thoughts determine our attitudes. Once again, your thoughts and feelings cause the results you experience in your life, not the other way around.

One of the most common attitude traps we all seem to fall into is keeping the past alive. And one important truth about the past is that it's always water under the bridge. This is one of the lessons we learn from God's supplying manna from heaven to sustain the Hebrews in the desert. And it's a lesson that those who recite the Lord's Prayer are reminded of every day. "Give us each day our daily bread" (Luke 11:3) teaches us two very important things. First, our Father is the source for everything. Bread, of course, does not mean merely food, but everything that nourishes us—mental, physical, emotional, spiritual, and financial sustenance. We may view others as the source—for instance, we may view our finances as coming from our job, but that's really only the manner by which our Father provides our finances. The Lord's Prayer makes it clear, though, that He is the source from which we get our nourishment. Second, we are asking for the bread daily. Like the manna from heaven that came down daily, yesterday's provision is gone and tomorrow's doesn't exist. All we have is today's. The present is a gift from God; how will you use today's gift?

Being present in the present is the only way to relate to the world as it is. So much of the time we exist enclosed in our little world composed of our past opinions and judgments about the people and circumstances of our lives or in the fears we have about the future. Over time these thoughts form the attitudes that become our habits of thought—our *habitudes.*

These habitudes are an important force in our lives.

If you keep going over and over a negative experience in your mind—as I did with the guy who cut me off on the parkway—your mind takes it in *as if it just happened again.* That's what I mean by habitude: it is when a thought is repeated to the point that it becomes a subconscious habit.

With such habitudes at work directing your imaginative energies, you can see how easily you can stay in a rut you don't really want. To get out of the ruts, you've got to break the hold these old habitudes have on your mind. You do that in exactly the same way you develop new beliefs and conquer old fears. Some experts call this "reprogramming," and that's precisely what it is: a disciplined and focused effort to build a new, positive program—a positive habit.

I call it *reinventing the past.*

The truth is, you actually can re-create your own past by redefining events that have already occurred, giving them a new and more powerful meaning.

How different would it be if I defined the guy who cut me off as a distraught friend, husband, or parent rushing to the hospital, instead of an inconsiderate jerk out causing danger with his carelessness?

In his book *The Seven Habits of Highly Effective People*, author Stephen Covey, speaking about paradigm shifts, tells one of the most powerfully moving stories I have ever heard in my life:

Covey is sitting on a New York subway one Sunday morning

when a man enters with his two kids. The children are as wild as can be, tearing up and down the subway car, grabbing people's newspapers and disturbing everybody. They are behaving like brats—and all the while, their father just sits there staring at the floor, oblivious to his children's rude, destructive behavior.

Finally Covey can take it no longer and remarks to the man that his kids are a mess and he ought to be more responsible.

The guy looks up at him with vacant, sad eyes and apologizes. Then he tells Covey that they have just come from the hospital where his wife—the mother of these kids—has just died . . . and he guesses the children don't know how to deal with that, so they are going a bit nuts, because they don't know what else to do . . . and again, he is sorry.

Whamm!

In an instant, Covey completely changed his mind—shifted his opinion and judgment of what was happening right in front of him—180 degrees.

Sadly, we often need such dramatic and even heartbreaking information to shift how we're thinking about things. There is powerful truth in the Native American wisdom "Walk a mile in the other man's moccasins before you pass judgment on him."

This is all part of developing a high-achieving attitude: Live each day as if it were your last, with passion and with excellence. "Go, eat your food with gladness, and drink your wine with a joyful heart, for it is NOW that God favors what you do" (Ecclesiastes 9:7, emphasis added). Yesterday is over and tomorrow may never happen. Today is all we have.

This is not a limiting belief; on the contrary, it is tremendously powerful. It brings an end to procrastination, and it marshals a passion and desire to achieve all the good things that we know we can achieve, because when we live each day as if it were our last, we live each day to its greatest potential.

"When Do I Die?"

A doctor once had a thirteen-year-old patient who needed blood to live. The doctor walked over to the girl's younger brother, who was sitting in the visitor's room, and said, "Davy, I need your blood to save your sister; will you help us?"

The little boy gulped, but said, "Yes," without hesitation. Davy would do anything to save his sister's life.

The doctor had Davy lie down on a table and started to transfuse blood from one of his veins directly into his sister. The family and the doctor prayed as they watched the girl in silence. Miraculously, in a half hour she was past the crisis. She would live. They were all elated, including Davy.

Then, through teary eyes, her brother asked, "Doctor, when do I die?"

Davy thought he was giving *all of his blood* to his sister and that he had agreed *to die* for her.

There's a great spark in all of us. The story of young Davy's courage can help all of us find that spark in ourselves.

I'm not suggesting you need to die or even be willing to die to be a success. These stories are powerful illustrations of beliefs and attitudes that simply cannot be beat. They show us what it is like to have the kind of passionate, courageous attitude that inspires effort, enterprise, or a life purpose—no matter how grand.

All of these attitudes lead us to an attitude of wonder. When Jesus said, "Let the children come to me, and do not hinder them, for the kingdom of heaven belongs to such as these" (Matthew 19:14), He was telling us that we need to be more like children. Of course we need the faith of a child, but there's more. We need to have a childlike attitude. Jesus taught His disciples to cultivate their sense of wonder and amazement—to be more like children. The great Jewish scholar and philosopher Abraham Joshua Heschel relates that unlike Solomon, if God were to offer him anything in the world, rather than wisdom he would choose wonder. In Heschel's teachings, wonder was the cornerstone of faith. Perhaps when Jesus taught children about the kingdom of heaven, He saw the wonder and amazement in their eyes. This sense of wonder is no doubt driven out of adults by years and years of "reality training." We need to get it back. Jesus shows us that we have a lot to learn from children.

How do you develop such an attitude? You already know that it's a matter of choosing your thoughts wisely, the things that inspire and encourage you. But what does it take to do that? We'll talk about that next.

6

SECRET

When we learn the ability to focus on anything, we will master that thing itself

Secret #6

Focus

The smallest bit of action separates the high-achievers from everyone else.

The difference between the Gold Medal and second or third place in an Olympic swimming event is often measured in only hundredths of a second.

How much better is the .300-plus hitter with a multimillion-dollar big-league baseball contract than a second-string .265 benchwarmer? One to two hits a week over the course of the season. That's all.

The winner of a major golf tournament like the Masters often wins by one stroke, a difference for the four-day tournament of *less than four tenths of one percent* better than the runner-up.

These examples are all from the world of athletic

competition, but they are indicative of the tiny-bit-better-than performance percentage that separates the winners from the losers in any field of endeavor.

The difference between success and failure is actually marginal—measured in a fraction of one percent *at the most.*

What is it that makes this difference? What quality does the winner have more of than the also-ran, second place, or loser?

Let me answer that with another story:

A master archer was in the forest with two students. As both students were notching their arrows, preparing to shoot at a target far off in the distance, the teacher interrupted them and asked each one to describe what he saw.

The first archer said, "I see the sky and the clouds above, I see the fields and grass beyond. I see the different trees of the forest—oak, beech, pine, poplar, and maple—and I see their branches. I see the leaves. I see the target with its colored rings. I see . . ."

The teacher stopped him mid-sentence and said, "Put down your bow, my son. You are not ready to shoot today."

He then questioned the second archer, "What do you see?"

The student replied, "Nothing save the goal at the center of the target, teacher."

"Then let your arrow fly," the teacher directed. And it did—dead-on in the very center of the target.

The difference between the two students' state of mind? *Single-minded focus.*

And the Blind Saw Anew

I want you to do a demonstration of focus with me that I learned from Og Mandino, one of the most inspirational writers and speakers of our time. Og wrote, among many other titles,

The Greatest Salesman in the World, a book that has sold over 20 million copies in over a dozen languages.

In one of Mandino's speaking presentations he asks someone from the audience who requires glasses to come up and join him on stage. The person removes his or her glasses and attempts to read a page from the newspaper. Of course, it's impossible for that person to see the words.

Then Og hands him a white three-by-five card with a tiny pinhole in the center. That's what I want you to do, even if your vision is clear. Take a white card with a pinhole in the middle and look through it at a page of small, what designers call "mice-type," which would normally be difficult for you to read or see clearly. Hold the card out in front of you a couple of inches from your eye and move the page of copy back and forth until it comes into focus.

The fascinating thing is this: almost anyone, no matter how poor his or her eyesight, will be able to read every single word through that tiny hole. The type will appear as clear for you as if you had perfect 20/20 vision.

Why? *Focus.*

That little hole causes your eye to focus. It cuts out all the extra stuff you don't really need to see, bringing all the power of your vision to bear on a small, focused point, which dramatically increases your ability to see the letters and words. That's what a pinpointed focus can do in any aspect of our life or work.

When you learn the ability to focus on anything about yourself, you will master that thing itself. Focus your thoughts and master your mind. Focus your emotions and master your heart. Accomplishing all of this will make you a master of possibilities and a master of life.

Mastering your mind is the key. Once we train our focus on our goals and desires, our mind acts like a heat-seeking missile, leading us through all the lessons we need to learn, through all the trials, tribulations, and celebrations necessary for us to arrive at precisely where we want to be. This is true for as long as we *maintain our focus*. When Peter saw Jesus walking on water, he asked Jesus to call him over, realizing that if He called him, he too would be able to walk on water. Jesus called Peter, and Peter walked on water—for a time. Do you know what happened next? Peter "saw the wind, he was afraid and, beginning to sink, cried out, 'Lord, save me!' " (Matthew 14:30). Why was Peter afraid all of a sudden? After all, he was doing it! He was walking on water! The answer is *focus*. While Peter was focused on Jesus, he was able to walk on water. As soon as he let his focus wander, he started to sink. Such is the power of focus.

Yet most people don't maintain their focus. Why not?

I want you to do a little experiment with me. Read over the following statement. Do it quickly and read it just once.

FINISHED FILES ARE THE RESULT OF YEARS OF SCIENTIFIC STUDY COMBINED WITH THE EXPERIENCE OF MANY YEARS OF EXPERTS.

Okay, now I want you to read it again, only this time count the number of F's in the text. Give yourself fifteen to twenty seconds to do this.

How many F's did you find? Three? Four? More? If your answer was three or four, go back and reread the statement, but this time look for the number of times you encounter the word *of.*

There are actually seven F's in the statement, and in a typical group of people who've never seen this demonstration before, the majority notice only three F's. This is because they don't focus on the *letters* in the statement. What gets in the way of their ability to focus, even with clear, specific directions, and even with very straightforward, black-and-white information, is that something disables or distracts their focus.

Most of us learned to read phonetically—and "of" appears as "ov" in our mind's "ear." Because we learned to read that way, and because we all tend to read by speaking the words aloud in our heads—and because we are creatures of habit, and because we make assumptions about nearly everything in our lives, and because we lack real and true focus uninterrupted by our constant self-talk chatter—interpretations, meanings, opinions, judgments, and editorializing—we don't see what is staring us in the face. We miss the correct number of F's.

And this is truly an in-your-face lesson, not necessarily polite or kind, but the kind of *wake-up!* we all need now and then.

You and I have no hope of success unless we can honestly and truly focus our attention *on the task at hand*—whatever that task

FOCUS ON THE TASK AT HAND.

may be. And there is much un-learning, much baggage, much habit that we must discard, replace, or refine before we can approach mastery of the life skill of focus.

Just for fun, here's another test. Read the following familiar passage quickly:

> Mary had a
> a little lamb

Did you catch that one? My guess is that you did.

After doing this dozens of times on a flip chart in front of a roomful of people, I can tell you that 80 percent of the time people don't see the two a's in "a . . . a little lamb." I think the reason you saw it now was that you were more attentive and focused because of the previous exercise. And that just shows you how easy it is to keep a keen edge on your focusing ability. Like everything else, all it takes is a little practice.

Fellowship

It's vital that you find a group of peers—I suggest between four and six, including yourself—with whom you can discuss all your challenges and together seek solutions to your problems and develop how best to optimize your opportunities. You will find that five or six minds together have the total sum of much more than those five or six minds. They are the equivalent of one super-mind. For me, this was never truer than in my new-found faith in Jesus. Tuesday morning Bible study and Wednesday evening prayer and fellowship have been of tremendous help, support, and value to me.

If you've ever wondered how a church service, prayer meeting, or workshop can be so powerful and exciting, this is why. There aren't simply one hundred people there. There are thousands of *relationships*. And if all those relationships are equally engaged in the same uplifting possibility, the lid can come off that room with ease. There is power in "being like-minded, having the same love, being one in spirit and purpose" (Philippians 2:2). Jewish law goes as far as dictating that prayer in groups of ten has special significance. It is not by accident that Jesus' disciples "all joined together constantly in prayer" (Acts 1:14), because there is fellowship, power, and intensity in togetherness.

Travel back with me to first-century Jerusalem. It's the time when Jews from all over the world gathered together in Jerusalem to celebrate Pentecost, when God gave the Torah to the Jewish people around fifteen hundred years earlier. But this Pentecost was different. This Pentecost, all the followers of Jesus got together in one place, bound together by a common faith. The book of Acts describes the event: "When the day of Pentecost came, *they were all together in one place.* Suddenly a sound like the blowing of a violent wind came from heaven and filled the whole house where they were sitting. They saw what seemed to be tongues of fire that separated and came to rest on each of them. All of them were filled with the Holy Spirit and began to speak in other tongues as the Spirit enabled them" (Acts 2:1–4, emphasis added). Unity—togetherness—was an essential element that paved the way for the coming of the Holy Spirit. Readers of the Old Testament will recognize that the same "togetherness" was experienced at Mount Sinai when God first gave the Torah to the Jewish people, when all of Israel encamped as one. Pentecost teaches us the power of a synergistic relationship. Pentecost signifies the divine revelation of God to Israel on Mount Sinai and God's divine gift of the Holy Spirit to those who follow Jesus. It is through the Holy Spirit that the early followers of Jesus were strengthened by God to fulfill their purpose and bear witness to God's love—bringing healing, hope, help, and faith to people who so desperately needed it.

Whose Mind Is It, Anyway?

What do you do when you have a negative, non-supportive thought?

What I used to do was focus on it, get wrapped up in it, become enraptured by it, as if I were going to make love to it— and that's a big mistake, because thoughts breed like rabbits. What I'd get when I entertained those negative thoughts was just more of the same.

For example, I'd start thinking about finances, and the next moment my wonderfully imaginative mind would wash over me like a stormy sea with wave after wave of negative, depressing, sad, no-possibility *junk!* And I never separated these thoughts from myself. I *was* what was negative, bad news, worthless, and all the rest.

Be very clear about this: *You are not your mind!* Good thoughts, bad thoughts, whatever—you are not those thoughts. Thoughts are something you *have*—like you have fingers and toes—not something you *are.* The connection between your thinking and who you are is that the results you cause to come about in your life over time are the product of your habits of thought.

Once you learn to focus your mind, the experience changes: those bogie-person thoughts come up, you notice they are there, but you focus instead on what you *want* to be thinking about, and the limiting thoughts simply disappear. At least for a moment. Chances are, they'll be right back, holding on for dear life.

Focus again on what you choose to have in mind. And keep doing this and doing it and doing it and . . . Sometimes, this back-and-forth wrestling match may seem like it will never end. But it does and it will—and it will actually do so faster than you would ever expect. *The mind is very teachable.* That is its true nature.

Simply focus: focus on what you choose to think . . . to feel . . . to say . . . to do. That's the key to shaping your own mind. What's more, there is no other way to live successfully with passion. Without focus, life really is a hard road—and a hopeless one.

In fact, that's a good definition of hopelessness: *the inability to focus on your goals and dreams.*

How do you acquire focus? Again, the same way you get to Carnegie Hall: practice, practice, practice.

As with the archers I wrote about earlier, single-minded focus on a goal is the way it's done. If you have many different goals, then you may need to practice shifting your focus from target to target. That's okay. Take it one at a time. There are some people who can stay focused on many projects at once, but I don't—and I don't think that works for most people, either. Single-minded focus is a skill all successful high-achievers have developed.

The place to start is with your mind and your thoughts.

Be aware of your thoughts. Inspiring thoughts can stay. Limiting thoughts are asked to leave.

Do this any way that works for you. Shoot down the thoughts you want gone. Say, "Stop!" Slash them to little pieces with a sword. Coax or sweet-talk them into going away as you would a little child who finds him- or herself in the wrong place at the wrong time. Whatever style is yours and you are comfortable with and good at, use it—as long as it works. Just stop the negative thoughts.

Then replace them with something you choose to think about.

Pray. Talk with God. God is with you and wants to help you. Learn to hear that still, small voice of truth.

You know, there are some people you just don't want in your home—right? So you don't let them in. Or if they're already inside, you ask them to leave. It's the same thing with thoughts. Kick the thoughts you don't want out of your mind. Like a diplomat or like a six-foot-six bouncer—it's up to you. Just make sure the unwanted thoughts are gone! Your mind is your castle. It's up to you to have around the kind of thoughts you want to hang around with.

If you wish, you can substitute the word "magnify" for focus. When faced with any situation, it is our choice what we focus on, what we magnify. My favorite example of this is when the angel Gabriel approached Mary and told her that she was going to have a son, who was to be conceived by the Holy Spirit. Can you just imagine all the conflicting emotions she must have been feeling when the angel told her this? Mary was a young, devout Jewish woman who knew exactly what everyone around her would think. She was also engaged to marry Joseph! What a scandal there could have been, and she could have faced the death penalty by stoning! Mary could have focused on all of that. She could have focused on all the trouble that was headed her way. But she didn't. Instead, she said, "My soul magnifies the Lord" (Luke 1:46 NKJV). She made God bigger in her mind than anything else, bigger than all her challenges. She magnified God to the point of blocking out from her vision all her fears, and she rejoiced. Mary teaches us a great lesson about focus.

The more you encourage those inspiring thoughts to take the place of the unwanted ones, the easier and more naturally they will become the predominant thoughts you have in mind all the time. Practice, practice, practice. That's all there is to it.

Prayer—written, thought, spoken aloud, or listened to—is a powerful ally in this focus-training process. Remember that the key is listening to the voice of God.

Focus works.

And what does it take to be focused?

Commitment. Yes, the "C" word. Let's focus on that next.

7

SECRET

Once we are committed to something, it happens

Secret #7

Commitment

> *"If you do not stand firm in your faith, you will not stand at all."*
> ISAIAH 7:9

A chicken and a pig were having a discussion. The chicken said, "I am committed to giving one egg every day."

"That's not commitment," the pig said. "That's just participation. Giving bacon, now that's commitment!" And the fact that a committed Jew is willing to use a bacon analogy shows just how committed I am to you!

Commitment doesn't ask how. Commitment just is. When Jesus called Peter and Andrew and said, "Come, follow me" (Matthew 4:19), they immediately did so. They didn't ask how. They just did it. You know the Nike ad: *Just do it!*

Of all the quotes I've heard or read concerning commitment, this one from W. H. Murray in *The Second Himalayan Expedition* inspires me most:

Until one is committed there is always hesitancy, the chance to draw back, always ineffectiveness. Concerning all acts of initiative, there is one elementary truth, the ignorance of which kills countless ideas and splendid plans: that the moment one definitely commits oneself, then Providence moves too. All sorts of things occur to help one that would never otherwise have occurred. A whole stream of events issues from the decision, raising in one's favor all manner of unforeseen incidents and meetings and material assistance, which no man could have dreamt would have come his way.

I have learned a great respect for one of Goethe's couplets: "Whatever you can do, or dream you can, begin it. Boldness has genius and power in it."

Isn't that wonderful?

Is there anyone who wouldn't love to have "all manner of unforeseen incidents and meetings and material assistance" on your side to help you along your journey toward success?

As simply as I can write it: Nothing happens without commitment. Commitment is the secret ingredient in every recipe for success. Once you are committed to something, it happens. No matter how long it takes, no matter what else happens, *no matter what.* That's the power of commitment. It's truly awe-inspiring!

Commitment Is When You Know

I want you to have an experience of commitment that really brings home what commitment means. So do this with me: Ask yourself, "Will my children [and if you don't have kids, use your spouse, your parents] ever starve to death?"

Take this question seriously; what is your answer?

I have *never* met *anyone* who said anything other than "No! Never! Not a chance!" And they say it immediately, apparently without any thought, with no hesitation at all.

Now, here's the interesting thing: the truth is, *you have nothing to back up your making that statement.*

The truth is, you really don't know what's going to happen tomorrow—or two or two hundred tomorrows from now. How could you possibly control the future? You can't. There is absolutely no evidence whatsoever that your kids (spouse, parents) will not starve to death, and yet you will state with total certainty that it will *never happen to them.*

How can you do that?

You can do it because you are *committed* to it. That's all. There is nothing more to say.

This is most powerful when you understand that God is sovereign and in control. It seems like a paradox. But it's not. Faith is the most powerful commitment builder.

> COMMITMENT IS THE SECRET INGREDIENT IN EVERY RECIPE FOR SUCCESS.
>
> ✳

That is commitment at its clearest and most compelling. It has nothing to do with *how* a thing will or will not be accomplished. Commitment is simply, powerfully, and without question, what you say *will* be done. The how of it all doesn't matter—*at all*—to the making of the commitment itself. Commitment has nothing to do with *how.* Commitment is what will happen—*no matter what.*

To What Are You Committed?

I'm going to make a bold assertion: What you have in your life right now, who you are in your life right now, is exactly what you are committed to—no more and no less.

Like belief, attitude, purpose, and all of the other qualities we've been writing and thinking about in this book so far, commitment itself has no color of its own. The color of your commitment is the color you give it. You can be committed to failure or committed to success. It's up to you.

You are *always* committed to *something*. The only question is, to what?

If you are more committed to your comfort than you are to achieving your goals, you *will be* comfortable—and you may or may not accomplish your goals. In fact, you might be *so* committed to your comfort that your goals become impossible, for there are times (most times, really) when we must get out of our comfort zone in order to reach for our aspirations.

Have you ever spoken in front of a sizable group of people? It's considered by most psychologists to be the number one fear of all time. Why do you suppose that is?

It's because most people have a huge, even monstrous fear of *looking bad.* Can you imagine anything worse than making a fool of yourself in front of hundreds of people? Would you be willing to be introduced with great fanfare to a big audience and then bomb, let them all down? Not me—and I'm certain, not you, either.

So what's the real problem here?

The problem is what the speaker is committed to. In the case of people who are scared to death to speak in front of a group, it is that they are committed to *looking good,* to doing it right, to not blowing it. They are locked in their comfort zone, and that's what they're really committed to—comfort.

What if, instead, you were committed to inspiring and encouraging everyone in the room—would that make a difference?

I promise you, it would. It has for me.

My career requires that I speak to large groups of people. At first, that scared my socks off. I was not in my comfort zone at all. And the reason I was so frightened was that I was more committed to doing it right and to looking good than I was committed to the men and women who'd come to see and hear me or to what they needed and wanted. I was interested in their thinking well of me. I wanted to be "good"—but not for them, really, for myself. I wanted to be liked, appreciated, and recognized. Important, even—dare I say it?—famous. It was all about me, my ego. That's what I was committed to.

When I finally got the message to commit to serving the audience, to inspire and encourage them and commit to their success more than to my own, I became a successful speaker. Before that time, I was too committed to me, myself, and I to be of much use to others.

Commitment is powerful. Whether for you or against you, it is, as always, up to you.

Have you ever met anyone committed to failure? I have, far too many times for my liking. And when you see a person who is committed to success, you sure can tell, can't you?

Have you ever seen an entire company or enterprise committed to success? It's amazing. (Remember the Nordstrom sales clerk? That's commitment!) You can almost feel their commitment. And it's not just superficial optimism and rah-rah, either. You just know they're going to succeed. And the reason you know that is that they are living and working out their commitments.

Do you remember the children's story *The Little Engine That Could*? I read that recently to my daughter. She loves it when the little engine begins chugging up that long steep hill, pulling the circus train behind it, affirming again and again, "I think I can . . . I think I can . . ." That little engine is *committed*.

Everyone is committed to something. The apostle Paul said, "You have been set free from sin and have become slaves to righteousness" (Romans 6:18). You can't have it both ways. You're either committed to one or the other. But make no mistake—you ARE committed to one or the other.

Most people are committed to convenience and comfort. To what are you committed?

Winners are committed to success and high achievement. To what are you committed?

Here's a great question: "How do I get committed?"

The Meaning of Commitment

First, let's have a clear understanding of what commitment really means.

Commitment is not necessarily a do-or-die affair; you don't have to throw yourself onto railroad tracks in service of your goal to prove you're committed to it. And you don't need to commit hara-kiri if you fail to reach a declared goal when or how you said you would.

When you are committed to something, you simply agree to play full out—win, lose, or draw. If you commit to making ten sales calls to new people this week, and it's Friday afternoon and you've met with only nine, you don't trot off to play eighteen holes of golf with your buddies or girlfriends. You go for that tenth call. Why? Because you said you would. More important, don't push aside your commitments to family. If you promised to show up for your son's Little League game or your daughter's dance recital, don't let business get in the way of that family commitment. Commitment is as simple as giving and keeping your word. Doing your best. Commitment is doing what you said you would do whether you feel like it or not.

Do you remember baseball player Reggie Jackson? Reggie's nickname was "Mr. October" because that's when the World Series is played—and no matter what, Reggie would come through in those championship games. Once he hit two home runs in a World Series game with a 104-degree temperature and a bad case of the flu. That's why Reggie is in the Baseball Hall of Fame. Mr. October, Mr. Commitment.

Do you remember when President Kennedy committed the entire country to landing a man on the moon in only ten years?

"I believe," Kennedy said, "this nation should commit itself to achieving the goal of putting a man on the moon before this decade is out."

Crazy, no? At the time it sure was. America was way behind the Russians in the space race, but the Eagle landed with a giant step for mankind and right on schedule, too. America, the land of the free—and the committed.

Our commitment will be tested, sometimes severely tested. When God told Abraham to sacrifice his son Isaac—that was a serious test of commitment! God told Abraham to "take your son, your only son, Isaac, whom you love, and go to the region of Moriah. Sacrifice him there as a burnt offering" (Genesis 22:2). That was one of the greatest tests of commitment the world has ever seen. And it foreshadows the single greatest commitment. Isaac, while carrying the wood for the burnt offering, asks his father a legitimate question: "The fire and the wood are here, but where is the lamb for the burnt offering?" (Genesis 22:7). Abraham answered, "God himself will provide the lamb for the burnt offering, my son" (Genesis 22:8). And God did, but not right away. In verse 13 we see that God provided a ram, not a lamb. However, Abraham didn't lie to Isaac. Abraham was speaking prophetically. It was in that same region, where two thousand years later God provided the Lamb of God who takes away the sins of the world. And just like Isaac, Jesus carried the wood—His cross—to offer us eternal life. Abraham knew that someday God would provide the Lamb in that region of Moriah. And Jesus, with his dying breath says, "Father, into your hands I commit my spirit" (Luke 23:46).

Obviously, this is no ordinary commitment, but what I want you to understand is that no commitment is ordinary.

Scratch just beneath the surface of any successful leader, from any walk of life or enterprise, and you will find the common thread of commitment in all of them. That's *why* they are leaders. People will follow those who are committed to a future of unlimited possibilities.

Leaders Leverage Power

One of my favorite biblical episodes is when God tells Moses to take off his sandals when he is approaching God on Mount Sinai (Exodus 3:5). God is teaching Moses a very important lesson about leadership. Shoes protect us from feeling the hurt and the pain of everyday life and living. But when we take off our shoes, we feel every pebble, every step. A leader must feel the experiences of those he's leading.

Jesus came as a new Moses, and the parallels are uncanny. Just as Moses was almost killed as an infant by the decree of Pharaoh, so, too, was Jesus' life threatened by the decree of Herod. Mary and Joseph had to escape Herod to save the life of the baby Jesus, and they went down to Egypt. As Moses led his people out of the bondage of slavery, Jesus leads us out of the bondage of sin.

The story of Jesus' baptism in the waters of the Jordan is another powerful example of leadership. Jesus could have entered the water alone, when nobody was there, but he chose to enter "when all the people were being baptized" (Luke 3:21). Jesus teaches us that to be an effective leader, we must totally identify with the lives of those we lead. And the number one key to effective leadership? You got it—service! For an in-depth study of leadership, I recommend you read *The 21 Irrefutable Laws of Leadership* by John Maxwell. For now, one last thought on the subject that's worth repeating: "The greatest among you will be your servant" (Matthew 23:11).

The fast lane on the highway of success is the lane of leadership because accomplishment through others is the key to success. This secret to leadership is summed up by a statement attributed to Andrew Carnegie: "I would rather have 1 percent of the efforts of 100 people than 100 percent of my own."

Why? Because leverage works. You can achieve one hundred times more through a team or network of people than you can ever do all by yourself. No man or woman is an island, and the nature of people is that they will do what you do. And they will do what you say if you are a person who keeps his or her word. In other words, if you are committed. The apostle Paul tells us to "Be *imitators* of God . . . as dearly loved children, and live a life of love, just as Christ loved us and gave himself up for us as a fragrant offering and sacrifice to God" (Ephesians 5:1–2, emphasis added). Have you ever noticed that children will mimic you—to the point you will want to pull your hair out? This is something we need to understand and be conscious of. Paul instructs us to imitate Jesus. It's especially good advice considering that people are watching—primarily our children. And people will imitate us. They will not necessarily imitate our words, but our actions. In other words, it's not what we say but what we do that impresses.

Leadership is the fast lane. People will follow you, if you are committed.

You must make a commitment before you ask for one. Commit to your dream the way a baby commits to walking. The child tries and tries and tries again until he or she walks. There is no maybe, no stopping, no comfort zone, there is only doing—walking.

Remember, we do not get paid for what we know, we get paid for *what we do* with what we know. We don't get paid for *whom* we know, either. We get paid for *what we can accomplish* with and through whom we know. And the *doing* of both of these, and anything else that matters, requires commitment.

Ed McElroy of US Air once said, "Commitment gives us new power. No matter what comes to us—sickness, poverty, or disaster—we never turn our eye from the goal."

Stew Leonard is the owner of "the world's largest dairy store" in Norwalk, Connecticut. His store began as a 1,000-square-foot, mom-'n'-pop retail operation, and has grown to over 100,000 square feet, with annual sales of over $100 million *from just one store!*

Early on in his business, Stew placed a three-ton rock beside the front door of his store. Chiseled in the rock is the following statement:

Rule #1: The customer is always right.
Rule #2: If the customer is ever wrong, re-read Rule #1.

That's Stew Leonard's commitment—carved in stone for all his customers to read. Why is the motto chiseled in rock? "Because," Leonard says, "it will never change."

Woody Allen once said, "Eighty percent of success in life is just showing up." True, perhaps, but "showing up" isn't all there is to commitment. It's the other 20 percent that rules and has the real power and makes the difference between failure and success. That 20 percent is commitment.

As I said before, commitment isn't necessarily a life-or-death matter. If you make a commitment and play full out and don't get the goal, you're not going to have to give up your firstborn child. When you are committed, you just play the game *as if* your child or something else that really matters to you were on the line.

The great football coach Vince Lombardi once said:

> There is only one way to succeed in anything . . . and that is to give everything. I do, and I demand that my players do. Any man's finest hour is when he has worked his heart out in a good cause and lies exhausted on the field of battle . . . victorious.

It's about commitment.

One more quote, from Walter Cronkite: "I can't imagine a person becoming a success who doesn't give this game of life everything he's got."

Please understand—commitment is not just for leaders! While the last section of this chapter focused on leadership, commitment is a principle for all of us. We must commit to being a good parent, spouse, role model, employer, employee, teacher, student, or anything else we pursue.

Take a moment now to go back and review your values and purpose, and also take a look at your beliefs. Then make a list of the top five commitments you are willing to make right now.

What are you committed to doing?

What kind of person are you committed to being?

What five things would you tell the world you are committed to right now?

And remember, don't give a thought to how you will accomplish these commitments. There'll be time enough for that later on.

Write your five commitments below:

1. _____
2. _____
3. _____
4. _____
5. _____

Do you know what one of the biggest payoffs is of being committed to something? Persistence. Now, many people would say that persistence is a tool, a means to an end. I say it's a *reward.* Marriage is a great example of how persistence is a reward. King Solomon wrote, "I am my lover's and my lover is mine" (Song of Songs 6:3). That kind of commitment that lasts forever is not easy, but it is its own reward.

One of the most cherished qualities of any associate or friend with whom I've developed a relationship over the years is persistence. Without it, you're sunk. "If anyone would come after me, he must deny himself and take up his own cross daily and follow me" (Luke 9:23). Jesus teaches us that commitment is something that must be renewed daily. The skill to stick to it and with it brings more joy and success than almost any other ability I know of.

Persistence, truly, is its own reward.

People often ask me, "Well, okay, but how long must I persist?"

Just think about that question for a moment. Do you see that it is an oxymoron—a concept that contradicts itself? It's like saying, "I like to be consistent—sometimes."

Very simply, you must persist until you succeed and reach your dreams. Everybody's dreams are different, and no one knows how long the gestation period is for any dream. What we do know, however, is that if you keep focused and committed, you MUST succeed. There is no way to fail unless you literally give up. And since the only way to fail is to give up, if you persist and do not give up, *you will succeed.*

The biggest problem most people have with success is that they quit before they achieve it. Did you know that 80 percent of all small businesses fail in their first year, that 80 percent of the rest don't make it to year five, and that 80 percent of those will never see year ten? Frankly, the biggest problem facing most entrepreneurs is that they quit before payday.

Think about that one, too, for a moment. If you've ever experienced a failure in your life, take another look at it and ask yourself, "Did I quit too soon? What's the possibility that if I had persisted, I would have succeeded?" Chances are excellent that you would have.

Again, persistence is its own reward. It comes from commitment and in turn strengthens it. Persistence is the opposite of giving up, and giving up is really nothing more than a bad habit—a habitude.

It's important to replace the bad habit of giving up with the good habit of persistence. Remember, the only way to get rid of a bad habit is by replacing it with a new and better one. And all it takes to enforce a new habit is twenty-one days of repetition.

Isn't it interesting that the only way to build the habit of persistence is through persistence? A lack of persistence and a lack of commitment can only result in feelings of indifference, indecision, and procrastination.

Here's a favorite quote of mine from Calvin Coolidge that speaks powerfully of persistence:

> Nothing in the world can take the place of persistence.
> Talent will not; nothing is more common than unsuccessful
> men with talent. Genius will not; unrewarded genius is

almost a proverb. Education will not; the world is full of educated derelicts. Persistence and determination alone are omnipotent.

Commitment in action is determined and persistent.
Commitment is relentless patience.
Commitment is what makes the difference.
Commitment requires focus.
Commitment requires positive belief.
Commitment requires a positive attitude.
Commitment requires purpose.
And all of these—focus, belief, attitude, purpose—require commitment.

What's the key to building a powerful commitment? That's next. It's called *desire*.

8

SECRET

The only way we get anything is if we *really want* it

Secret #8

Desire

T he fine art of perseverance is beautifully expressed in the popular reggae song whose lyrics I don't remember, but you'll get the basic idea:

If you really, really want it you can get it.
If you really, really want it,
If you really, really want it,
You must try . . . try, try, try . . . try, try, try . . . try, try, try.

Now, as you know, I'm not a big fan of the word *try*—so my appreciation of this song just goes to show I'm finally acquiring the skill of being flexible.

What I love about these lyrics is the driving repetition: "If you really, really want it." I don't think the song would have been anywhere near as good if the lyrics instead were:

You can get it if you sort of want it, or
You can get it if you halfway want it, or
*You can get it if you, well, don't really want it, but somebody
else said it was a fine idea, and besides, it's an appropriate thing to
want for someone with your income and standing in the community,
and what's more, your mother would approve, as well, and . . .*

You get the idea.

The only way you get anything is if you *really want* it.

Sort of want, halfway want, don't really want—those other
less-than, quasi-wants just won't cut it. If you're going to "succeed at last," you've got to *want* to.

Wanting to Want To

"Delight yourself in the Lord and He will give you the desires of your heart" (Psalm 37:4). But you've got to really want
it. It doesn't say He will give you your passing fancies. You will
get your true desires. There's a big difference. Real wanting unfortunately has a number of impostors to contend with. The
cleverest of these false wants is *wanting* to want to.

I know so many people who suffer from this. It's so debili-
tating and limiting because it looks for all the world as though
they really want something—but they don't.

I've watched people spend their whole lives *wanting to want
to* live somewhere else, work at some other career, do this, have
that, but it's all an illusion: busywork masquerading as productivity.

Wanting to want to is avoidance, holding back, fear of the
unknown. It's stating goals that sound good but not really being
committed to them. It's confusing aspirations with wishful
thinking. I suspect it's as much fear of failure as anything—a
form of procrastination that allows the person to look good in

the process of doing nothing productive, save going through the motions. And that's very sad. "Hope deferred makes the heart sick, but a longing fulfilled is a tree of life" (Proverbs 13:12). Real desire has something inspired about it.

Real wanting is something very different. It's a powerful inspiring urge, and as such, there is something divinely inspired about it.

I have never been one to hold with those spiritual and personal growth practices that maintain the only way to an "enlightened life" is through ridding oneself of all desire. I think desire, genuine wanting, is a gift from God, a powerful and compelling tool for accomplishment. Desire is a human birthright and very much directly linked to (indeed, responsible for) all the extraordinary and exciting progress we people have made over the centuries of our existence on this planet. Of course, we've taken some wrong turns, made some mistakes and errors in both judgment and action. But it is our *desire*—especially when it appears collectively—to right those wrongs that will inspire the process to a new and better result.

DESIRE, GENUINE WANTING, IS A GIFT FROM GOD.

The Power and Force of Desire

Like any other quality we've been thinking about here, desire has no color of its own. As always, that's up to each of us individually. Desire for more than is appropriate, or for greater than you deserve, is greed. And desire for less than you deserve is often an expression of a self-defeating, no-possibility habitude, born of low self-worth and low self-esteem.

Clearly, genuine desire is powerful. Developing the ability to harness its strength for good and not for harm is the challenge.

The Jewish sages often state that when you have a strong will for something, whether good or evil, God will lead you in that path. As a negative example, the Midrash (Leviticus Rabbah 12:1) warns against the harm of alcoholism: "If a person drinks too much wine, he will end up selling all that he owns to keep up his addiction to drinking." The Midrash then relates a story of a man who spent so much money on his habit of drinking that his children were worried they would soon be penniless. When he was drunk, they tied him up and took him out to a cemetery. They hoped that when he became sober he would be shocked to find himself in there and would become aware of the dangers of drinking too much. That same day a caravan carrying vats of wine passed near the cemetery. The caravan was attacked and traveled as fast as it possibly could. One of the large barrels it was carrying fell off and landed right next to the head of the drunken man. When he woke up from his drunken stupor, he was surprised to find the faucet of the barrel right next to his face, and he kept drinking right there in the cemetery. The events that led this person to find wine in a cemetery were so unusual that they were almost miraculous. The sages comment that even if a person's true desire is evil, God leads a person where he wants to go. The sages further comment that this principle is all the more true when a person has a strong will to do what is good.

Robert Fritz, in his book *The Path of Least Resistance*, gives practical insights into the accomplishment process. I'm particularly impressed by his explanation of how we get what we desire.

When we have a desire for something, and what we have at present is different from the fulfillment of that desire, there is a natural tension that develops. This tension is subject to the natural law that tension seeks resolution.

Picture a stretched rubber band. The tension in that rubber band acts almost as if it *wants* to relax, to resolve the tension and go back to its resting state. And so it is when we desire something we do not have. There is a tension, stretched between our current condition and the desired condition that seeks to be resolved. The bigger the desire, the greater the tension.[1]

The fun part for me is to see that this tension is not only a natural occurrence but it is also the force we use to get what we want—whether or not we are aware of its presence. As long as we continue to encourage and maintain that tension, it's there for us, naturally and powerfully bringing our desire into being. Fritz shows that while people often experience such tension as something stressful, it can be used and experienced as the powerful inspirational force it really is.

Now, let's do something really fascinating with Fritz's rubber-band imagery.

Think of what you have now in your life as the end of the rubber band that's in your left hand, and of your desire as the end in your right. Now, stretch the rubber band out to represent the difference (i.e., the distance) between the two.

With your present condition and your desired-for future being pulled toward each other by the taut rubber band, what's going to happen next? How will you influence *in which direction* that tension resolves?

For the sake of illustration, let go of the right side. The tension relaxes the rubber band over to your left hand, correct? This would be like *letting go of your desire*. That's one way to resolve

[1]Robert Fritz, *The Path of Least Resistance* (New York: Ballantine Books, 1989).

the tension: Give up your dreams, forget about what you want. When you do, *snap!* What you end up with is just what you already had—your present condition.

In this case, letting the rubber band's tension relax means resignation—nothing's changed, your dreams are futile, you give up and stick with the status quo. And many people accept that condition in order to escape the tension that is naturally produced by having dreams and aspirations unfulfilled.

But what if you do it the other way around? What happens if you let go of the left-hand end of the rubber band? Now what remains is your desire, right?

Here's the really fun part: What you have now, what Fritz calls "current reality," will do one thing you can always count on. *It will change.* Everything does. Everything changes. So if you hold on to your desire, if you make it strong through the Success Secrets you're reading about here—belief in yourself, an up habitude, focus, letting go of your fears—you can direct and even accelerate the changes in your current circumstances, moving from what you have now to what you genuinely desire!

Think about it for just a moment. What you have now will change—that's a given. It's changing right now as you read this. If you hold on to and make powerful the desire for what you want, natural tension will tend to resolve naturally in favor of your desires.

There are two keys to this: telling the truth about what you have now, and telling the truth about what you desire. While affirmations, as we discussed earlier, could be powerful, lying to yourself is dangerous. So be honest with yourself. Then keep the tension alive, so that its natural power is working for you to accomplish your desire.

Isn't that fantastic?

Once you have the intense desire to achieve whatever it is

you want to achieve—and inspiration itself is your ally—you are unstoppable. If your desire is truly intense—what we call *burning desire*—and you are single-mindedly aiming toward your goals, no one and nothing can sidetrack you. "Ask and it will be given to you; seek and you will find; knock and the door will be opened to you. For everyone who asks receives; he who seeks finds; and to him who knocks, the door will be opened" (Matthew 7:7–8). The key is to know exactly what you are asking for and seeking and what you really, really want!

Building Rapport

Once you've cultivated an intense and burning desire, you can communicate this desire to others. And when you do that, you supercharge the entire accomplishment process. The more people you enroll in your desire, the more inspirational power you have to accomplish your dreams.

You transfer your beliefs to others in three ways:
1. through your words
2. through your voice inflection
3. through your body language

These three forms of communication combine to form the skill we call "building rapport."

When you have learned the skill of establishing rapport with unlimited numbers of people, you have developed a literally infinite variety of avenues for the experience and expression of joy, happiness, and success in your life and work—and perhaps most important, *in theirs.*

In essence, building rapport simply means establishing the most commonality and comfort possible in a relationship.

Most human beings have a fascinating behavioral quality: *We like people who like us.*

I know that's true for me. I would have a very hard time warming up to someone who had just said to me, "You know, Hirsch, I think you're a fool, and I frankly don't like you one bit. And what's more, your mother dresses you funny."

As Abraham Lincoln said, "If you would win a man to your cause, first convince him that you are his friend."

We spend time with and feel comfortable with those people who share our interests and passions. Even people who have difficulty talking to strangers will do so easily if there is an obvious commonality between them, such as the fact that they are both riding mountain bikes, or that they're both wearing jazz dance shoes or baseball caps from the same team.

Most people establish rapport with words—by asking questions to reveal areas of common interest or personal similarities. But this is a far more limited basis for rapport building than it might seem because of the often-overlooked fact that *words mean different things to different people.* We all have our own definitions for words and unique interpretations for the same set of "facts." Take five people to view the same event, and you'll have five quite different descriptions of what happened.

However, when you use rapport-building skills, you can guarantee making a connection with others. Can you see value in being able to establish rapport instantly in a variety of personal and professional encounters? It really is powerful.

Perhaps the greatest lesson on rapport building comes from the apostle Paul: "Though I am free and belong to no man, I make myself a slave to everyone, to win as many as possible. To the Jews I become like a Jew, to win the Jews. To those under the law I become like one under the law (though I myself am not under the law), so as to win those under the law. To those not having the law I become like one not having the law (though I am not free from God's law but am under Christ's law), so as to win those not having the law. To the weak I became weak, to win the weak. *I have become all things to all men* so that by all possible means I might save some" (1 Corinthians 9:19–22, emphasis added). Because Paul's belief was great, his mission to win the lost so clear, his focus so intense, his desire so uncompromised, he had to become all things to all people. Paul put himself in their position, walked in their shoes, empathized with them. And it worked. Paul became the world's greatest missionary. We can do the same in our fields of work.

Let's take a brief look at some rapport-building skills you can use easily and immediately.

Mirroring and Matching

It's important to realize how little of our communication is composed of words. In fact, according to some widely respected research conducted years ago by the Pacific Institute in Seattle, our communication is actually 93 percent nonverbal. That is, words themselves comprise *only 7 percent*—about one-fourteenth!—of our total communication.

If words represent such a small part of our communication, where do the other thirteen-fourteenths come from? More than in any other way, people judge you and make decisions about how they think and feel about you based on your *voice inflection and body language.*

When you mirror and match the inflection and body language of the person you're meeting with, you develop instant rapport—no matter what is being said. People are most open and comfortable with other people who are *like them.* Mirroring and matching is a practice whereby you observe and adopt some of the dominant characteristics of the person with whom you're speaking.

You might think this technique is too obvious or "phony," that you will come off as strange or even be perceived as mocking the other person. But that's not the case. What we're doing here is actually quite subtle, and it communicates almost entirely on a subconscious level.

The truth is, *we mirror and match each other all the time.* When people around us start to yawn or laugh, we often start to yawn or laugh. It's something you already do naturally and automatically, at least to some extent. My purpose here is simply to have you recognize that fact and focus on it—that you bring it out of the realm of the subconscious so you can begin to use mirroring and matching with awareness and discipline to achieve the results you're after.

Let's start with your voice.

Your Voice

Your voice inflection comprises 38 percent of your communication with others. There are four aspects of your voice that can be looked at separately: tone, tempo, volume, and vocabulary.

Tone. The tone of your voice is a quality apart from how fast or slow, how quietly or loudly you talk. Here are some examples of different tones: excited, dry, laid back, thoughtful, hurried, enthusiastic. What you *call* the tone of a person's voice is subjective and unimportant. What matters is to observe the tone being used and to emulate that same tone in your conversation with that person.

Tempo is the speed with which a person is talking. Your goal is simply to match the pace and pattern of the other person's speech.

Volume, like tempo, is self-explanatory. Speak softly with soft-spoken men and women, loudly with those whose volume is greater.

Vocabulary. Notice key words the other person uses and use them in your conversation, as well. Especially important are words that give you the person's predominant thinking orientation, such as when he or she says "I think" or "I feel" or "I see" or "I hear what you're saying." Although you may be a "thinker," when you're with someone whose orientation is one of "feeling," match that in your conversation by shifting what you normally would say from "I think" to "I feel."

I normally speak quite quickly and fairly loudly. I also tend to say "I think" a lot. And I often use a number of other key words you might recognize from reading this book: passion, focus, choice, purpose, encourage, inspire, power, service, and success, among others.

Now, if you came up to me, speaking fast, excited, and in a strong "presentation voice," and said, "Peter, this is great! I think we can really inspire lots of people to greater success, to surpass their limitations and fears by focusing on having a choice in all that they do and say, by connecting them with what they're truly passionate about in their lives . . ." I would conclude that you are a very intelligent, high-integrity person who's really up to great things in your life. I would like you and respect you immediately, and want to spend time with you talking and sharing more ideas together!

Back in law school, long before I learned about any of these communication skills, I had an amazing experience that I wondered about for years afterward—until I discovered the mirroring and matching technology.

I was a top student, used to getting all A's. We had a midterm exam in tort law, and as I emerged from the classroom I knew I'd aced the exam. I even had the thought that I had been so brilliant they were surely going to invite me to be on the faculty.

I got a C-minus! I couldn't believe it! Me, Peter—L-for-Lawyer—Hirsch with a C-minus on my law exam. I was stunned!

I went immediately to the law library and checked out every book and paper my tort professor had ever written. I studied them for the remaining weeks of the semester. When it came time for the finals, I knew every word, phrase, and manner of expression my professor used—and I put them all into the exam paper.

How did I do? You can guess.

This time I got an A.

I'm convinced that there was no difference between the substance of my mid-term and that of my final. All that changed was the fact that my *expression* on the final matched that of my professor. Therefore, he was more comfortable with me and probably thought to himself, *"Ahh, now there's a student who really understands the material!"*

Mirroring and matching is the most powerful way in the world to have people on your side, open and wanting to share with you who they are and what they're up to.

Your Body Language

Body language represents 55 percent of your communication. There are so many aspects of body language you can mirror: gestures, posture, people's relationship to the space around them, their breathing, touch, movement, facial expression—and much more.

As you begin to mirror and match another person's body language—the movements of the hands in gesture, his expressions, posture, how near or far away he stands or sits in relationship to you—you'll discover an amazing thing. You will actually begin to *feel the way the other person is feeling.*

Stop, Look, and Listen

Obviously, the importance of mirroring and matching tells us something interesting about our habitual communication styles: Most of us talk too much!

It's true: People generally talk much more than they listen. But the fact is, we learn *only* when listening; we learn nothing by talking. "The heart of the discerning acquires knowledge; *the ears of the wise seek it out*" (Proverbs 18:15, emphasis added). What King Solomon is teaching us is simple—LISTEN!

If you're going to succeed in any enterprise, you've got to care about people. It's a matter of leadership. Perhaps you've heard the expression "People won't care about how much you know till they know how much you care." It is quite true; and the best way in the world to show people how much you care— and the quickest way, too—is by listening.

There is nothing more effective at raising people's self-esteem, self-confidence, and sense of self-worth, than showing them we care; and we do this primarily by listening—*really listening.*

That isn't as easy as it might sound. Focusing on another person means shutting down everything on your own list, paying complete attention, and hearing every single word the other person says. Some people call this "listening without an agenda." It means setting aside your own concerns, your evaluation-in-process of that person and of what he or she is saying, and simply listening.

There's a great expression that speaks directly to this point: "The mind is like a parachute: it's of no use unless it's open."

Listening to people—openly, not thinking about what you are going to say next, without inside-the-mind comment—is the most effective way to show people you care and the very best way in the world to learn and encourage.

Make a commitment to be aware of the importance of listening to people. Be aware of body language—yours and theirs. When appropriate, lean forward, smile, and put interest and attention in your eyes. This lets people know that you are fully present with them, affirming their importance to you, being enrolled in their self-worth (and yours, too, for that matter), and giving them confidence in you.

To be a leader, it is vitally important to let people feel they can open up to you—and the best way to do that is by *asking questions.*

The Right Questions

There are two types of questions, open-ended and closed. Open-ended questions can lead to all sorts of places; they literally open up possibilities. Closed questions lead nowhere. They ask for nothing more than one specific answer—usually yes or no. They are like emotional short circuits.

We gain very little information from closed questions: "Well, Bob, did you like the training?"

Whether Bob answers, "Yes, I did," or "No, not really," the conversation still goes *clunk!* You really haven't moved forward at all. This is because closed questions are not structured to reveal people's genuine desires. Open-ended questions do just that: "Bob, what was the best part of the training for you?"

It is only when you understand other people's desires that you will be able to see how you can benefit them. And always remember, that's what people care about: how you can benefit them. What your value is to them.

The worst mistake that anyone who deals with people can make is to talk facts, figures, and statistics. Nobody *really* cares about them. People want benefits, and benefits alone. People are after value—we are all value-driven homing devices.

Last year hundreds of thousands of refrigerators were sold in the United States. And guess what. Not one person wanted a *refrigerator!*

What did they really want? They wanted fresh food and cold food. They wanted the convenience of food stocked up near them so they could fix meals without having to go out to shop each time. They wanted the *benefits* that a refrigerator would bring them: fresh vegetables; food that lasts longer; cool, refreshing drinks; ice cream, and so forth.

Do you know how many drill bits are sold every year in this country? Millions. Do you know what every one of those drill bit buyers are really after?

They don't want drill bits. They want holes.

When you ask questions, ask those that give you the greatest opportunity to really listen, questions that cause people to tell you what they want, what their feelings are, questions that reveal their desires and how you can help them achieve them.

Asking open-ended questions also provides you with a fringe benefit: you will find yourself living everyday life with much more interest and involvement. People are like snowflakes: there are no two exactly alike. If you give people time and attention, if you listen to them, if you reveal their desires, they will open up to you. They will come into partnership with you in a combined effort to achieve all your goals and theirs, as well. That kind of powerful, inspiring relationship with others is the key to success.

With proper communication skills; targeted, consistent

focus; commitment; and an intense, burning desire, your mind, functioning with the unerring accuracy and perseverance of a salmon returning to its spawning ground, will take you to any and all of your goals.

And that's exactly where we're going next.

9

=== *SECRET* ===

The purpose of goals is to focus our minds and our imaginations

Secret #9

Goals

his is the most difficult chapter for me to write. Not because the subject matter is unfamiliar to me, and not because I haven't practiced it. I have. But something more important must come first. Here goes: We MUST make sure our goals are in accordance with the will of our Father. When we pray, "Your will be done," we must mean it. We can't mean "Your will be done, unless it's not what I want." That won't work. There's a wonderful Yiddish expression that says, "Man makes plans, and God laughs." If we are moving in a direction in our life that goes against the will of God, it's called a recipe for frustration and disaster. "Many are the plans in a man's heart, but it is the Lord's purpose that prevails" (Proverbs 19:21). Unless you would rather swim against the current, plan your life in harmony with God's will.

Once you are comfortable that your desires are not opposed to God's desires for you, then you need to take action. Someone says, "If this is what God wants for me, let Him do it alone." We need to understand that our lives are a partnership. Jim Rohn tells a wonderful story of a man who was walking in the middle of a desert. All he could see in every direction was sand, for miles and miles. Finally, in the middle of the desert, he comes across a magnificent garden. He finds the gardener and tells him, "This is some garden here. You and God did a terrific job on it." The gardener thinks for a moment and answers, "I'll buy that. I couldn't have done this without God's help. The garden needed the wind and the rain and the sunshine. But I'll tell you something—you should have seen this place when it was *just* in God's hands."

It's a partnership, and we have to do our part.

There's one more thing to consider before we get into setting goals. You can't start with goals. If you skipped straight to this chapter, go back to the beginning and especially focus on the chapter about purpose. You can't start with goals; you must start with purpose. The reason why most goal-setting programs fail is because they're not linked to a purpose you care about. You can have all manner of goals, and I'll ask you, "Are you really going to do this?" You say, "Yes." That's like most New Year's resolutions. What's going to make you do it when the going gets tough? What's the overriding purpose to which your goals are linked? Then we can get into goals. With all of those disclaimers, let's begin.

The purpose of goal-setting is to focus our minds and our imaginations.

Do you remember what you were doing when you were

fifteen? If someone had asked you at that age (and it's quite likely someone did—at the least, a high school guidance counselor), "What do you want to do with your life?" do you have any idea what your answer would have been?

If someone asked you that today, do you know what your answer would be?

Do you have an answer? You must! Otherwise you wouldn't be here. The question really is, are you consciously and specifically *aware* of what that answer is?

In the 1920s, when John Goddard was fifteen years old, he answered that question quite specifically. In fact, he wrote down all the goals he had for his life. He wanted to

- run a mile in five minutes or less;
- climb Mt. Everest;
- live with primitive people in the Sudan;
- visit all the countries of the world (there are 141);
- read both the Bible and the *Encyclopedia Britannica* from cover to cover;
- play Debussy's "Claire de Lune" on the piano;
- pilot a submarine;
- write a book; and more.

In fact, there were 127 entries on his list of goals!

Today John Goddard is one of the most respected and well-known explorers in the world. He has achieved 108 of his original 127 goals. He has visited 113 countries and intends to complete the remaining part of that goal by seeing the other 28. He continues to pursue all the goals he has yet to fulfill—exploring the entire length of the Yangtze River in China, walking on the moon, and many, many more exciting adventures.

Such is the power of goals.

But where does this power come from—and how can you

use it to inspire success for yourself and others?

As the great New York Yankees philosopher Yogi Berra once said, "If you don't know where you are going, you might wind up someplace else."

Your life and work can be either a Sunday drive or an on-purpose, by-design journey to your true destination—your destiny. By the way, "destiny," "destination," and "destine" all come from the same Latin word, which means *to establish* or *to make fast and firm.*

That's what goals are all about. They focus us, they make our desires firm and fast. Goals establish the direction for your attention and awareness; they give your imagination a laser-like one-pointedness and focus your entire arsenal of inspirational tools on the task of turning your dreams into reality.

Goals and Fellowship

At one of my fellowship meetings, we discussed the topic of goals. When asked, I flipped open my notebook and read from my list of goals. Before I share with you some of my goals, I want to tell you that what you are about to read is NOT where I began in my goal-setting process. When I began, I had nothing tangible with which to start. Financially, I also had nothing. In fact, one of my early goals was to "get back to zero." I was so far below zero that zero became a goal. Emotionally, I was, for lack of a better word, new. I had a new beginning with Jesus in my life. My goals began with very simple declarations: I will read the Bible every day. I will thank God for His love and mercy every day. And so on. Eventually I piled up some successes. That led me to create longer-reaching goals. Please, don't be intimidated by the list that follows—it was years in the making.

Here are some of them that I read from the list of more than one thousand goals I've written down for myself:

- I will affect millions of lives by bringing people to Jesus.
- I will always tithe with pre-tax dollars.
- I will deliver talks at churches all around the world.
- I will deliver a talk at Harvard University.
- I will deliver a talk at Oxford University.
- I will deliver a talk at Congress.
- I will deliver a talk at Hebrew University.
- I will speak in Carnegie Hall.
- I will learn and become fluent in Japanese.
- I will learn to play the piano.
- I will learn how to ballroom dance.
- I will learn how to fly jets.
- I will bicycle along the Great Wall of China.
- I will visit Russia.
- I will visit Eastern Europe.
- I will visit outer space.
- I will own a home in Jerusalem.
- I will work out six days a week for thirty minutes each day.
- I will teach people lessons from the Bible.
- I will buy my wife a gift every month.
- I will never leave home without kissing my wife and daughter and telling them I love them.
- Every day I will walk closer to God than the previous day.

When I finished reading and looked up, the rest of my group applauded vigorously, shouting, "Bravo! Bravo!" I blushed in response, not because I am shy about my goals, but simply because whenever you share your goals with others—or they share theirs with you—there is a power about it. Our goals inspire people.

Goals are very special in that way. That's because goals inspire power. They have a life of their own, and when you share them with the "right" people, those people tap into your goals and get their own infectious energy from them. Right then and there you've enrolled another person with inspirational and encouraging power to join you in partnership for the accomplishment of your goals.

I should warn you right up front: The chances are good that you'll encounter people who react negatively to your goals. They'll shake their head and do their "grave dancing" routine. They'll talk "no-possibility" to you. But don't ever let that throw you off track. They are just people who have trouble being in the presence of real courage, determination, and desire. The truth is, your goals probably scare them.

Do you know why many people don't have goals? Four reasons:

1. *They have not been sold on any single idea.* This is because they have NO BELIEF that they can achieve their goals.
2. *They don't know how to set goals.* It's what I call a "technical problem"; they truly DON'T KNOW HOW to set and get their goals.
3. *They are afraid, because setting goals involves risk.* What if they don't get what they want? They're AFRAID TO FAIL. Remember how important looking good is?
4. *Because of lack of self-esteem and self-image, they don't think they deserve success.* They DON'T DESERVE SUCCESS? This is the saddest reason of all. Of course they deserve success! Everybody I've ever met deserves success.

If you've ever participated in one of the hundreds of personal development or personal growth seminars out there, you may have heard a workshop leader say something like "We're not going to fix anyone here. There is nothing to fix. Get off the thought that you're broken."

Well, I'm here to tell you that if you think for one moment you do not deserve success, *something IS broken!* *You do indeed require fixing.*

It may be acceptable to some people to walk around with the thought that we don't really deserve to succeed. Not for me! As far as I'm concerned, you *must* be a success, and that's all there is to it. There is no excuse for not living and working with a level of joy and accomplishment equal to or even beyond your wildest dreams.

If you're not *living with passion*—you are not living!

This time that we're living in has been called the "Age of Responsibility." I agree—and furthermore, that means that it's also the *Age of Freedom,* because freedom and responsibility are two seemingly opposite but actually complementary sides of the very same coin. If you're up for making a better world, if your life purpose has something to do with making a difference to people, with taking a stand for the highest possible quality of life—for yourself and for all the others with whom you come in contact—then *your success* is the single most important and powerful contribution you can make.

Remember Roger Bannister and the first under-four-minute mile? Your success will have the same impact. You can be the one that breaks the logjam of mediocrity that enslaves our world and propels us all into a future of indescribable beauty, productivity, and joy.

Let me explain what I mean by that.

In the areas of Canada where they do the majority of North America's logging, loggers use rivers rather than roads as their highways, floating the huge logs they cut down the river to the saw mills. Sooner or later, the logs get stuck in what we all know as a logjam.

Now, the interesting part is that although the loggers are

faced with hundreds, even thousands of these great trees tangled up in a hopeless, immovable traffic jam, they know there is one single log that, when moved the right way, will free up the entire mess and send all those trees floating freely downriver again. They call this one log the kingpin.

YOUR SUCCESS IS CONTAGIOUS.

❋

Is it possible that you are a kingpin? Bannister was. What would happen to the people around you if you were freed up to become a big success? Don't you think that would inspire and encourage them? I can promise you it would. I cannot count the number of times I've watched organizations and groups of people experience a breakthrough in performance, stemming from the success of one single person.

That's why you *must be a success.* Your success is contagious. You will inspire many people to greater levels of accomplishment and happiness in their lives and work simply by being successful yourself. Again, look at Bannister breaking the four-minute-mile barrier: hundreds and thousands followed him and even bettered his accomplishment.

People who don't think they deserve success have merely forgotten that they do. You can tell them: "What do you think— God put us here to be miserable? Wouldn't that be a great creation. Come on! Creation is a mega miracle, and you and I are its greatest achievement so far. Of course we're here to be successful!"

Perhaps the people who don't believe this have been worn down by unwanted circumstances. Maybe nobody's ever told them that they do, in fact, deserve success. So tell them! YOU DESERVE SUCCESS! It's both a birthright and a responsibility, and the greatest freedom you will ever experience. What's more, it's the perfect way to say thank you to our Father who put this whole program together for us.

Your success is the gift you've come to life to give. *Of course*, everyone has the right to *expect* success.

However, expectations alone, with nothing else to inspire them—without a solid structure for accomplishment, without a design of thought and action—remain just hollow expectations. And unless that condition changes, chances are quite good that they'll never be fulfilled.

Expectations are powerful! Goals are powerful! And step one for making your goals and expectations real is to write down your goals.

Write Down Your Goals

A famous study was made of the Harvard class of '53. In this study, researchers discovered that only 10 percent had established goals at all, and that only *3 percent* of the men and women in that class had written down their goals.

Twenty years later researchers interviewed those same class members, who were now involved in careers and families. They quickly determined that the 3 percent who two decades earlier had written down their goals were now worth more in economic terms than the entire remaining 97 percent of the class combined! Now, I know that economic success isn't everything—but it certainly is a revealing and immediate way to measure the power of having written goals.

The truth is, until your goals are written down, they're not really goals; they are dreams and wishes. And if wishes were fishes, it'd be the rare angler who catches the really big ones.

Without a magic lamp, without action on purpose and by

design, wishes rarely come true. I love fairy tales. Most people do. They're the lottery of literature. But I will not bet my life and the well-being of my family and my world on a trail of breadcrumbs scattered in the forest.

Writing your goals down in black and white forces you to focus on them. Then you will commit to them.

Furthermore, as I wrote before, it's important to share your goals with like-minded people—your champions. "Therefore encourage one another and build each other up, just as in fact you are doing" (1 Thessalonians 5:11). All of us need people on our side.

Do you know what a champion is? In days of old, when knights were bold, a lady had a champion. He was a shining-armor-clad character who defended her—life, honor, and all—against dastardly dragons, bad dukes, and any and all other negative assaults on her position or person. A champion is one who takes the field on behalf of another. Kings and queens all had champions, and you and I have them, too. Anyone who takes a stand for your greatness is your champion.

Do you want to know how to live a life of accomplishment, fulfillment, and success? Have lots of champions. And the way to do that is to share your goals with committed, believing people and develop powerful partnerships with them. Be their champion. Championing others is a powerful way to catapult your own success.

The Three Legs of Accomplishment

Accomplishment is a three-legged affair, and it requires all three legs to stand solid and strong. You know how strong a tripod is: it can support hundreds of times its own weight—yet take away one leg and it will instantly topple and fall. The three legs of accomplishment are:

1. Results
2. Growth
3. Fun

When you look at any of your accomplishments, you should be able to rate on a scale of one to ten what's true about them in each of these three areas.

A ten is perfect; nothing is missing. If you rate a given area less than a ten, then add to the score itself a statement about what's missing, which, when put in place, would make it a full-fledged ten. This will direct you toward any imaginative adjustments you need to make.

Too often people focus only on the results. But getting results without learning something or without having fun are incomplete. So is having fun without getting the result, or having fun without learning something new to help inspire you in the future. Accomplishment is all three: the result, growth, and having fun.

Results alone are not enough at all. Be very clear about all you want to accomplish and be sure in your goal-setting to include all those other things you want, as well as money or that new house or car. Especially important are goals about your relationship with God, learning and development, relationships with family and friends, and having FUN!

On your list of goals, make sure to notice where each goal has possibilities for fun, where the result is clear and concrete (which means *measurable*—and I'll say more about that shortly), and where you will be learning new and better ways of being and doing—that is, where the goal provides for growth and development.

Remember, we are human *beings*, not human *doings*;

goal-getting and accomplishment are more the result of who you are *being* than what you are *doing.*

Obviously, doing, taking action, is vital. But again, remember that results themselves are the consequence of *who you are;* your actions are the natural outcome of your beliefs, values, purpose, attitudes, fears, desires, thoughts, and habits of thought. Successful people, those who accomplish their goals, are being successful within themselves before they achieve the realities of success in the external, relative world of people, places, and things.

My point here is simply this: The most profound thing you can do to bring any and all of your goals to successful manifestation, is to BE a successful person.

By believing, having an "up attitude," and putting into regular practice all the other Success Secrets we're exploring in this book, you can *become* the kind of person who accomplishes his or her goals.

Goal-Setting Specifics

Let's get back to the specifics of goal-setting and goal-getting. Setting and getting goals follow certain rules.

Rule #1: Your Goals Must Be Concrete and Have Measurable Results

Wishy-washy goals—aren't. Airy-fairy goals aren't, either. Wishes and dreams and it-seemed-good-at-the-time ideas aren't goals at all.

Goals are solid and clear—and they can be measured and expressed in concrete terms. *I'm going to be a lawyer* is more dream than goal. *I'm going to graduate from law school* or *I'm going to get my law degree* is quite different. Do you see how the second one is more measurable, more concrete as a goal? I'm going to get my law degree by June 30, 2003, is even more so.

It's really quite simple: If it can't be measured, it's not a goal.

I'm going to be thin and trim. Really? How thin? How much will you weigh? How many inches will you be around the waist? Around the hips? Be specific with your goals. Clear and concrete goals have power. Foggy goals are for people who aren't willing to lay it on the line. If you have a vague, unspecified goal, no-body can say you failed if you don't reach it. Have courage. State powerful goals you can measure.

Rule #2: Set the Goals You Really Want

Don't make "process goals," and by this I mean, don't make goals that are really only steps along the way to a goal. Of course, all goals always lead to new goals—but make your goals results that you actually want to achieve, not ingredients in the mix or part of the process. Go for the ultimate result you have in mind.

Having money, for example, is not a powerful or effective goal. Recall from our discussion of values: why do you want the money? What do you want it for? Like digging down to the core of essential values, go to the core of a goal. *That's* the goal to write down.

Rule #3: Give Your Goals an ETA

"ETA" means estimated time of arrival, what some people call a "by when." This is another instance where specificity in-spires. No time frame—no reality. Until you assert your goal as an expected result by such-and-such a date, it's a wish, not a goal. (As a famous advertisement for a still-prosperous savings & loan company once said, "Wishing won't do it—saving will.")

Make sure your ETA is reasonable, or you may set yourself up for failure. "Finish law school in one year" may be exciting, but it's not reasonable.

Rule #4: State Your Goals As Positive, Present-Tense Accomplishments, Complete With Feelings

Avoid expressing your goals as negatives or as wants off in the future somewhere. And include an emotional payoff to supercharge your goal.

Let's take, for example, "I will quit smoking." Instead, you might state it this way: "I am living smoke-free—and I feel fantastic!"

Which of these two expressions stirs up some passion? Which of those two seems most likely to succeed?

"So by when will you be feeling great because you're completely smoke-free?"

"April 1, this year."

"Great!"

The more compelling your goals, the more passion they call forth from you, and the more likely it is that you will hold them up and champion them, and that others will, too.

Working With Goals

Once you've established your goals, you'll need to work with them to bring them into being. One reason to write goals down is that this brings them closer to reality. Having an inspiration or imaginative idea, giving it focused thought, and then writing it down, are powerful steps in the success process. Do you see how each one is more concrete, more "real" than the one before?

Once your goals are written down, read them every day. If

you want to, say them out loud as you read them. If you've designed your goals as I suggested—positive statements complete with feelings—then your goals are powerful statements, and speaking them aloud adds to their reality.

Have both short-term and long-term goals. Don't be afraid to use your imagination. Let your goals stand as real possibilities, not just a better version of the same old thing, but brand-new conditions and realities you've never accomplished before.

Remember, only when you aspire to excellence in your life can you be free from mediocrity. Because one of your goals must be constant growth and improvement, always ask yourself: *What can I do differently? What can I do better? What can I do BEST?*

One key to knowing if your goal is on track is to check whether the goal makes you a little nervous. If your goal makes you sweat a bit, then chances are it's a really good goal—one that will stretch you and cause you to learn new and different skills as you go through the process of accomplishing it.

You've heard the term "movers and shakers." Here's what that phrase means to me: *People who are really moving are always shaking a little!* Great goals, big goals, bring out the best in people.

It's been said if you want to clear the fence and you aim for exactly that, you might make it and you might not. But if you shoot for the moon, no matter what, you're bound to clear the treetops. The bigger your goals, the better.

Remember the stretched rubber band? The bigger your goal, the more natural tension there is available to inspire you to bring it into existence.

Where the Getting Gets Good

Setting goals is one thing. Getting your goals is another. Effective goal-getting involves two simple steps:

1. Reverse goal-setting
2. Consistent focused action (CFA)

Reverse goal-setting is simple. Look at your goal as a completed present-tense accomplishment, and then ask yourself, "What had to happen just before that was achieved?" Write down your answer.

Now ask the question again about the specific accomplishment you just wrote down, and write *that* answer down. Then do it again and again and again, until you end up right where you are now, at your starting place. When you do this, what you'll have is a written plan that breaks down your goal into a series of doable steps. Through reverse goal-setting, even the most ambitious goal can be broken down into a series of smaller, progressive goals.

Once you have your goal laid out on paper in front of you in a sequence of sub-goals, you can then design a strategy of actions to take. I recommend the consistent focused action, or CFA. Looking at your goal and all the sub-goals that need to be achieved to accomplish it, you'll be able to see what one thing you could focus on and do consistently that would bring you your goal.

Let me give you an example:

One of my goals was: *This book will be published by the summer of 2001.* (By the way, I missed this one by about six months—and that didn't matter to me at all. The goal was real, and it served to make this book happen!)

Now, reverse goal-setting: What had to happen just before the book was published? It had to be printed. And before that? It had to be laid out to what printers call "camera-ready." And before that it had to be designed and typeset, and the cover designed, and before that it had to be proofread, and before that it had to be edited, and before that there had to be a completed manuscript, and before that . . .

This process was a real eye-opener. When I started, I had no idea what it would take to publish a book, but after doing the reverse goal-setting, I had a really clear idea! Once I had the steps all laid out, I could see that in order to finish the book on schedule, I would have to write a chapter a week. My CFA was to write one chapter a week. That required another CFA, which was to write two hours each day, Monday through Friday. Then I discovered that I don't write very quickly. I spend a lot of time going back over things and thinking about better ways to say or to illustrate something, so I quickly increased my two hours of writing to four hours per day. That worked fine.

I had my goal, and it had me moving—and shaking! I knew how important the book was going to be for people, so all my passion was called upon. And I had a step-by-step plan of action that would bring me my goal in the time frame I had planned. There were some things I didn't expect that backed me up a bit. But all in all, this book was completed, and it took a little less than twice as long as I expected. On the accomplishment scale, it's a twelve! (Remember, that's on a scale of one to ten.) I got the result, learned a tremendous amount, and had a ball.

I knew clearly what it would take, and that took the anxiety out of my project. (I think we're more frightened by what we don't know than by what we do know. Remember the poor fellow who chose the firing squad over the door to the unknown?) The whole process of having my goal, a one-at-a-time sequence of steps on the way, and my series of CFA's all down in black and white took away any fears and replaced them with specific actions I knew I could take.

There may be a better way than reverse goal-setting and the CFA to get a step-by-step map of what to do, but I haven't discovered (or developed) it yet. It's powerful stuff.

Goal-setting is okay. Goal-getting is fantastic! I highly recommend it to everyone.

Rewards

One of the things I did to keep the whole process going and flowing was to give myself a reward every time I completed a sub-goal. This is one element that's missing from most goal-setting and goal-getting systems—your rewards *along the way.* Some long-term goals take years to accomplish, so getting rewards for completing successful steps along the way is important for maintaining your passion and focus.

Every time you develop a specific goal, make it a part of the structure that you will grant yourself a reward upon successful completion of each sub-goal as well as of the ultimate goal. And, very important: *Make your reward something you would not normally do or give yourself.* For instance, if you go out for dinner often, don't make that your reward! (However, if you generally stay home for meals, the reward of going out to eat may be just right.) New clothes, trips with the family—there are hundreds of special favors you can do for yourself that make the whole business of working on your goals more fun.

Appreciation and recognition are two of the most common of human values, so reward yourself *whenever* you do a good job, no matter how easy or small the accomplishment.

Helpful Hints

Along with writing down your goals and doing the reverse goal-setting exercise, here are some other valuable elements to identify—in writing:

- What obstacles will you need to overcome to complete your goal?
- What skills will you need to develop to complete your goal?
- Who are the people you'll need to speak with and the resources you'll need?
- What other knowledge will you need to reach your goals?

If you need help identifying your goals, think about the following two questions:

1. What Things Do I Value Most in My Life? Think about this question for as long and as hard as you need to, to feel clear and secure with your answers. They should determine where you want to go, who you want to be, what you want to do, and what you want to have.

2. What Have I Always Wanted to Do, but Was Afraid to Try? This one provides you valuable clues to parts of you that you may have buried away or filed under "N" for "no-possibility." It puts you in touch with essentials—your values and your life purpose. Children have a wonderfully simple question that gets to the heart of this: "What do you want to be when you grow up?" Sometimes that's a good question to ask ourselves!

Another great way to access these dreams and goals is to start the sentence, "Someday, when I have the time, I'm going to . . ." and then fairly quickly, without giving it a lot of thought, complete that sentence in as many ways as you can. Then take a fresh sheet of paper and do the same exercise, only starting out, "Someday, when I have the money, I'm going to . . ." You might be surprised—and pleased—at what comes out on the page.

Remember, people don't plan to fail—people fail to plan.

Goals are planned actions you can take that in a very short time can change your life for the better and forever.

Your goals are the productive offspring from the marriage of your life purpose and your values. They are inspiration itself expressed on a local, individual, human scale. In short, goals—making them up, pursuing them, learning from the process, and finally bringing them into existence—give meaning to life. So this is especially important: don't sell out. To get a million dollars and give up your dignity—that's called a bad deal!

To illustrate *meaning in life,* here's a favorite passage from a work by Edgar Lee Masters called *Spoon River Anthology.* In the book, Masters has the entire town speaking to the reader from their graves. Here's what one of the townspeople, George Gray, had to say:

> I have studied many times
> the marble that was chiseled for me—
> a boat with a furled sail at rest in a harbor.
> In truth, it pictured not my destination,
> but my life.
> For love was offered me and I shrank from
> its disillusionment;
> Sorrow knocked at my door, but I was afraid.
> Ambition called to me, but I dreaded the chances.
> Yet all the while I hungered for meaning in my life.
> And now I know that we must lift the sail
> and catch the winds of destiny,
> wherever they drive the boat.
> To put meaning in one's life may end in madness,
> but life without meaning is the torture
> of restlessness and vague desire—
> It is a boat longing for the sea and yet afraid.

You must not be afraid to unfurl your sails!

Set down your goals on paper. Read them. Take consistent, focused action to accomplish them. When you do, you will catch the winds of destiny and live the rewards of joy and adventure that come to everyone sailing the stunning seas of life.

Enjoy the ride! " 'For I know the plans I have for you,' de-clares the Lord, 'plans to prosper you and not to harm you, plans to give you hope and a future' " (Jeremiah 29:11).

We have been *gifted* with the dignity of choice

Secret #10

Choice

> "Choose for yourselves this day whom you will serve . . . but as for me and my household, we will serve the Lord."
>
> JOSHUA 24:15

T he tenth success secret is the simplest of all, yet it is the most powerful—for it is the one you must exercise to gain access to all the other nine.

It is simply the knowledge—not only in theory or in periods of reflection, but moment by moment throughout your day—that it is up to you. Unlike any other creature on the face of the earth, you and I have been *gifted* with the dignity of choice.

It's your *choice.*

It is through choice—not chance—that we forge our futures. We are all in possession of the power to shape our destinies, moment by moment, with choice. Choice is what differentiates us from all other creations of God. We owe it to Him to use the choice wisely. Ruth told her mother-in-law, Naomi, "Where you go I will go, and where you stay I will stay. Your people will be my people and your God my God" (Ruth 1:16). The historic effects of that one seemingly inconsequential choice are mind-boggling. From Ruth down through the ages comes King David; and from the lineage of King David comes Jesus. Never under-estimate the ripple effects of your choices.

I want to share a story with you that I first heard from Dr. Charles Garfield, about a young man named Henry Peterson.

Henry had a dream of being the very first person in his family ever to graduate from college. He applied and was accepted to Georgetown University.

Henry had another dream. He wanted to play college foot-ball. He never considered going pro; he just wanted to play for his college team. He tried out for the team and made it.

For four years Henry sat on the bench.

One week before the final game of the season, in his senior year, tragedy struck Henry's family. His father died. Henry was torn. If he went home, he'd let the team down; if he stayed and played, he'd fail his family.

He asked his coach for advice. The coach told him, "Go home, Henry. Your family needs you more than the team does." So Henry went home.

About an hour before the big game, who should show up in the locker room but Henry, suited up and ready to play! The coach, seeing him there, blew his top. "Henry," he shouted, "I thought I told you to go home!"

"Coach," Henry replied quietly, "I need a favor."

"What?!" replied the upset coach. After a moment, he cooled off and told him, "Anything, Henry. What do you want?"

"Coach, I need to start the game today."

"What!" said the coach, with some anger returning. "Well,

not *anything*, Henry. Look, you've sat on the bench for four years. I can't start you—"

"Coach," Henry repeated firmly, "just this once—please?"

"All right," the coach relented, "but the first time you compromise the team effort I'll take you out, Henry. It's nothing personal. The game is just bigger than you or me."

So Henry started—and he was *awesome*.

He blocked. He faked. He carried the ball play after play after play, gained over one hundred yards rushing, and scored two touchdowns on the way to helping his team win a resounding victory.

At the end of the game, the coach ran up, gave Henry a bear hug, and yelled, "Henry, Henry, why didn't you tell me you could play like that?"

"Did you ever meet my dad?" Henry asked in return.

"No, son," the coach said, "I never had the pleasure."

"Did you ever see my dad and me walking around the field for hours and hours, talking, arm in arm?"

"No, son," the coach said, then asked, "What's your point, Henry?"

"Coach," said Henry, looking at the older man with tears in his eyes, "my dad was blind. Today was the first game he was ever able to see me play."

Henry fulfilled his dream of being the first in his family to graduate from college—and he went on to build a very successful business career, as well. Henry points to that day and that football game as his shining moment, as the day his life changed for the better—forever. When asked, "Why?" Henry says, "Because that was the day I realized it was my choice to be a bench-warmer or a player."

Choice, not chance.

That's the key to *Success by Design*.

And please understand, this is not a choice you make once, after which you are done with it. The choice of *Success by Design* is a moment-by-moment opportunity. You will be presented with the choice again and again and again, thousands and even millions of times throughout your life. Each time it will be new and fresh. Each time you make a choice in favor of *Success by Design*, you will be energized, uplifted, electrified!

Choice is our greatest power. No one can ever take it from us. It is the ultimate gift and the ultimate freedom.

CHOICE IS OUR GREATEST POWER.

——— ✳ ———

So how do we make sure we are choosing wisely? What's the key to proper decision-making? Here's the key: Learn the value of pre-deciding. Our decisions determine our habits, and habit is the daily battleground of character. We must learn to make the decision before the situation presents itself. If you wait for a crisis to determine your values, you will have no values, but you'll sure have plenty of crises. Decide your values beforehand, before temptation arrives, and then remain true to your values. Decisions become easy when you know what you stand for.

Decision-making requires that you know your values and that you stay committed, because often decisions don't bring immediate change. But change will come—you can count on it!

There are really only two types of decisions we need to make: clear choices and tough ones. None of us should struggle with clear choices. We all know right from wrong, commitment versus compromise, anger versus love. Struggling here is more an issue of character than a challenge with decision-making.

So let's talk about how to make tough decisions. Pastor

Gerald Brooks teaches that we need to analyze our decisions in light of six tests.

The first is the *test of improvement.* Paul writes, " 'Everything is permissible for me'—but not everything is beneficial. 'Everything is permissible for me'—but I will not be mastered by anything" (1 Corinthians 6:12). Because something is lawful doesn't mean that it's either necessary or proper. Will it make me better (that usually means it will not be comfortable)? Also, will it control me? We've all chosen situations that have ended up controlling us. It's usually easier to get a hold of things than to let them go. Even things as obvious as a new house with a higher mortgage—is it worth it? What will you have to give up to meet the higher payments? How much more time away from your family will the additional work require? It's easier to get a hold of things than to let them go.

Next, *does it meet the test of influence?* "Be careful, however, that the exercise of your freedom does not become a stumbling block to the weak" (1 Corinthians 8:9). The apostle Paul is reminding us that we do not live in a vacuum. Our decisions do not affect us alone, but have an impact on others.

The third test is the *test of motive.* "Dear friends, if our hearts do not condemn us, we have confidence before God" (1 John 3:21). Simply put, am I being honest with God, others, and myself about my motives?

Another test is whether it *agrees with the moral will of God.* Is this decision in harmony with God's principles? An easy way to understand this is to ask if the decision is in agreement with or against the Golden Rule. If not, it's a bad decision—NO EXCEPTIONS! Situational ethics do not work. To act one way in church and another way in business is simply hypocritical. Either you accept God's principles and act accordingly in every situation or you don't. Along these same lines, we need to ask ourselves whether this decision will keep our priorities in line—God, family, life purpose, and work—in that order. If we have an incredible opportunity available to us with a 100 percent increase in salary, but it means moving the family to a place where there is no church and bad schools, is that really the proper decision to make? Will it honor your priorities?

Fifth is the *test of perspective.* King David's decision to have Bathsheba's husband transferred to the battle zone in order to get him killed after David had had his way with Bathsheba failed the perspective test. The prophet Nathan gave King David this test: "The rich man had a very large number of sheep and cattle, but the poor man had nothing except one little ewe lamb he had bought. He raised it and it grew up with him and his children. It shared his food, drank from his cup and even slept in his arms. It was like a daughter to him. 'Now a traveler came to the rich man, but the rich man refrained from taking one of his own sheep or cattle to prepare a meal for the traveler who had come to him. Instead, he took the ewe lamb that belonged to the poor man and prepared it for the one who had come to him'" (2 Samuel 12:2–4). Of course, David is understandably outraged and says the rich man deserves death. Then Nathan gives David the news: "You are the man!" (2 Samuel 12:7). David then understood that his actions with Bathsheba were less than honorable! His choice failed the test of perspective. Before you make the decision, what would you say if someone else asked you if they should do it? That's perspective. Have you asked for someone else's perspective?

The last test is the *shout-it-from-the-mountaintop test.* If everyone knew you were going to make this decision, would you make it? "For whatever is hidden is meant to be disclosed, and whatever is concealed is meant to be brought out into the open" (Mark 4:22). Here's the bottom line: If you wouldn't make the decision if others knew about it, then don't make it.

Choice. It's what separates man from beast.

All we must do is choose. Choose, and then keep choosing.

Given the choice, I know you will choose *Success by Design.*

Epilogue

The Problem

> "I have come that they may have
> life, and that they may have it
> more abundantly."
>
> JOHN 10:10 NKJV

After completing this book, you should know the skills you'll need to master *Success by Design* and how you can be successful in all your endeavors. Practice may not make perfect, but it does *make competent*, and then comes the confidence to act powerfully.

But, for many of you, there may still be one fundamental problem yet to solve that seems insurmountable. Let's take a look at it.

In the personal growth and leadership development field, as well as in any number of spiritual disciplines, many teachers and trainers speak about "non-attachment," a free and non-involved state in relation to the results of our actions—such as being non-attached to money, or outcomes, or people.

Well, I have a confession to make. I am attached, BIG TIME, to the results of my work.

Of course, I understand that not everyone who attends my seminars or reads my book will change his or her life for the better forever. But my commitment—and my intention and *expectation*—is not only that you get your time and money's worth from your efforts and mine, but also that I make a positive difference in your desire, ability, and actuality of living a successful life. I will not rest until that is accomplished.

Now, I've already done more than enough seminars and trainings in my life to see that there is an inherent flaw in even the most powerful and life-changing workshop, book, or tape experience. The next morning everyone goes back to work, back into the same lives they had *before* they got all that great new information and had those life-changing experiences and insights.

Did you know that over half of all first-time heart attacks occur between eight and ten *on a Monday morning*?! What does that tell you? It tells me that some people would rather die than go to work! It tells me that in the workaday world and life paradigms most of us are trapped in today, there is no room, no creative space for people to grow and approach their lives afresh and anew.

Whether you spent a weekend relaxing or recreating with your family, or attended a powerful life-changing seminar, or had some other experience that created a dramatic shift in your awareness, attitudes, and beliefs—let's face it: you still live, work, and exist in a culture and society that may offer little opportunity or encouragement for you to put into practice a *new you.*

You may have gotten a host of new capabilities and pos-sibilities from reading *Success by Design*, yet still find yourself in a context where circumstances seem to fight you at every turn—as if their mission were to prevent you from being the very best you can be in your life and work.

Has this ever happened to you?

Is it happening to you right now?

I have a solution to the problem that may fit you per-fectly; but first, a story:

> On a dark and stormy night, a battleship is return-ing home to port after maneuvers in the North Atlantic. The seas are stormy and gale-force winds are blowing, so the captain of the ship has remained on deck to see the vessel safely to its dock.
>
> Now, a battleship is a massive assemblage of hun-dreds of tons of metal and engines and guns and com-puters and technology—and people, over a thousand men and women. It's like a skyscraper on its side in the water. And tonight this particular skyscraper is tossing up and down in very rough seas.
>
> All of a sudden the signalman leans onto the bridge and says, "Captain, signal off the port bow."
>
> The captain has only one concern at this point: he asks, "Is she steady or moving astern?"
>
> If the signal is moving astern (toward the back of the boat), all is well; they are simply two ships passing in the night. But if the signal remains steady, that means they're on a collision course.
>
> "Steady, Captain," comes the reply.
>
> "Signal this," barks the captain. "We are on a colli-sion course; suggest you change course twenty degrees."
>
> The signalman does so, and the response comes

back: "Suggest YOU change course twenty degrees."

Now, it is quite rare for a naval captain to be addressed in such a fashion. But the captain retains his composure and, though a bit aggravated, commands his signalman to send the following: "I am a captain—change course twenty degrees!"

Again, the reply comes back: "I am a signalman second-class—YOU change course twenty degrees."

Now the captain is furious, and he roars the message, "I am a *battleship*. CHANGE COURSE TWENTY DEGREES!!"

And the signal returns: "I am a lighthouse."

There is a lighthouse of opportunity for you to live and work in a way that is congruent with the new beliefs, attitudes, desires, commitments, goals, and choices you've gotten from *Success by Design*. It's called turning over your life to Jesus Christ.

I have never found any system or structure in the entire realm of living life that by its very nature gives power to and rewards precisely what you and I have been studying together in this book—with the proven, powerful, and profound exception of life in Jesus Christ.

With Jesus you are free to pursue your desires and goals without the constraints of life as usual. You are free to live life without limitation. Life in Jesus is the only place where you can and should live beyond your means. We can believe beyond our means; we can love beyond our means. Why? Because God's love secures us. Three things we know for certain: people will fail us; places will discourage us; and possessions will disappoint us. That's fine. Actually, that's wonderful. We can be totally honest about our weaknesses and still be completely confident in God's love.

Life in Jesus Christ is a lighthouse to the battleship of passion—especially in the context of today's "apathy rules" picture.

There is not a single part of this book, not a subject or story that cannot be fully experienced and expressed through life in Jesus Christ—and I am not aware of another pursuit of any kind where the same is true.

Life in Jesus is a precious gift—and a free one at that! I am on a mission to turn millions and millions of people on to the possibilities of life in Jesus.

Life in Jesus isn't about how smart you are. It is about having desires and goals and being committed to them—and committed to having other people achieve their desires and goals and fulfill *their* commitments, as well. Life in Jesus is about expressing your values and life purpose; about conquering your fears; about upping your attitude and believing. It is about focus and, above all, about having and making choices that strengthen, inspire, and encourage yourself and others.

There is much more to know about life in Jesus Christ. Speak to the person who gave this book to you. Tell them you want more information about making Jesus the Lord of your life. More than anything else in this book, that is the one decision that truly matters. Everything else is secondary.

I urge you and encourage you to choose the only path that offers the opportunity to live *Success by Design*, not only in this life but also in the next.

Remember, it truly doesn't matter how much money you have, what kind of car you drive, or what kind of house you live in. It doesn't matter whether you drive a truck or fly rockets. Here's what does matter: Know that you are a child of God. Know that He loves you. Know that He wants to bless you.

As you implement these strategies in your life, please share your stories with us. If you have made the decision to invite Jesus into your heart, please tell us. If you're still thinking about that, please let us know. We want to pray for you. Contact our ministry at *www.peterhirsch.org*, and may God bless you.

My best to you,
Peter Hirsch

Secret #1:

Challenge

Secret #2:

Belief

Secret #3:

Purpose

Secret #4:

Fearlessness

Secret #5:

Attitude

Secret #6:

Focus

Secret #7:

Commitment

Secret #8:

Desire

Secret #9:

Goals

Secret #10:

Choice